WINE & DINE

WINE & DINE

CALIFORNIA FINE WINES
MATCHED WITH GOURMET RECIPES

RON BREITSTEIN
&
HENDRIK VAN LEUVEN

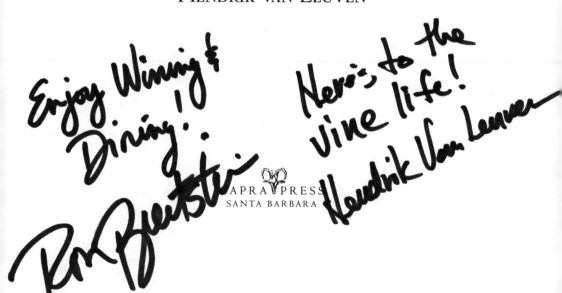

Enjoy Wining & Dining!

Ron Breitstein

Here's to the vine life!

Hendrik Van Leuven

CAPRA PRESS
SANTA BARBARA

Cover design, book design, image scanning and typography by Frank Goad
Cover photography by Roger Rosenfeld
Food styling by Sue White

LIBRARY OF CONGRESS CATALOGING-IN-PUBLICATION DATA
Breitstein, Ron, 1963-
    Wine & dine : California fine wines matched with gourmet recipes /
Ron Breitstein & Hendrik Van Leuven.
        p.   cm.
    ISBN   0-88496-410-8 (pbk.)
    1. Cookery, American—California style. 2. Wine and wine making—
California. I. Van Leuven, Hendrik. II. Title.
TX715.2.C34B74   1996
    641.59794—dc20   96-32400
                                                            CIP

CAPRA PRESS
P. O. Box 2068
SANTA BARBARA, CA 93102

To our wives, Paula Van Leuven and Suzanne Breitstein—who helped us keep on track, pushed us when needed, encouraged us when necessary, calmed us down when we were frantic, and believed in us throughout —we lovingly dedicate this book.

TABLE OF CONTENTS

GRGICH HILLS FUMÉ BLANC
Ahi Carpaccio Salad
—42—

LONG VINEYARDS SAUVIGNON BLANC
Involtini di Pesce Spade e Gamberi (Marinated Scampi and Swordfish a la Primi)
—44—

ROBERT MONDAVI WINERY FUMÉ BLANC, RESERVE
Savory Goat Cheese Cheesecake
—46—

ROBERT PECOTA WINERY SAUVIGNON BLANC
Zucchini Fritatta
—48—

SPOTTSWOODE SAUVIGNON BLANC
Roasted Chilean Sea Bass with Creamy Rock Shrimp Sauce
—50—

CHARDONNAY *52*

ACACIA CHARDONNAY, RESERVE CARNEROS
Veal Stew with Fresh Herbs
—56—

AU BON CLIMAT CHARDONNAY, SANFORD & BENEDICT
Lobster with Saffron Risotto
—58—

CAKEBREAD CELLARS CHARDONNAY
Sea Scallops with Warm Salad of Sweet Corn, Roast Pepper and Shiitakes with Chive Oil
—60—

CHALONE VINEYARD CHARDONNAY
Scallops of Striped Bass with Tomato
—62—

CHALONE VINEYARD PINOT BLANC
Oysters Rockefeller-Van Leuven
—64—

CHATEAU MONTELENA CHARDONNAY
Bo's Abalone Autentico
—66—

EDNA VALLEY VINEYARD CHARDONNAY
Chicken, Mushrooms, Cream and Tarragon
—68—

FISHER VINEYARDS CHARDONNAY, COACH INSIGNIA
Grilled Ahi with Cilantro Sauce
—70—

GRGICH HILLS CHARDONNAY
Chicken with Wild Mushrooms and White Wine Sauce
—72—

JORDAN CHARDONNAY
Corn Pancakes with Smoked Salmon Butter
—74—

KISTLER CHARDONNAY, DUTTON RANCH
Seared Whitefish with French Fries "Not Fried,"
Roasted Garlic Cloves
and Brandade
—78—

LONG VINEYARDS CHARDONNAY
Crayfish and Yellow Tomato Bisque
—82—

LOUIS M. MARTINI CHARDONNAY, RESERVE
Golden Coquille St. Jacques
—84—

ROBERT MONDAVI WINERY CHARDONNAY, RESERVE
Chive Cannellonis with Prawn
and Shiitake Filling
—86—

SANFORD CHARDONNAY, BARREL SELECT
Plush Pistachio Chicken Breasts
—90—

SIMI WINERY CHARDONNAY
Shrimp, Corn and Red Bean Salad
—92—

WILD HORSE CHARDONNAY
Fettuccine with Saffron Cream
—94—

RIESLING 🍇 96

LONG VINEYARDS JOHANNISBERG RIESLING
Papaya with Caviar
—98—

TREFETHEN NAPA RIESLING
Saffron Dungeness Crab Bisque
—100—

GEWÜRZTRAMINER 🍇 102

BABCOCK VINEYARDS GEWÜRZTRAMINER
Gingered Prawns
with Scallion Risotto
—104—

LOUIS M. MARTINI GEWÜRZTRAMINER
Roasted Cornish Game Hens
—106—

SPARKLING 🍇 108

"J", JORDAN SPARKLING WINE
Tuna Tartare
—114—

DOMAINE CHANDON BRUT RÉSERVE
Eggplant, Zucchini and Tomato "Tarte Tatin"
—116—

DOMAINE CHANDON ÉTOILE
Cheesecake with Strawberries Marinated in Sparkling Wine
—118—

IRON HORSE BRUT
Roast Chicken with Lemon and Olives
—120—

IRON HORSE BRUT ROSÉ
Charcoal-Grilled Rockfish with Green Onion and Tomato Relish
—122—

IRON HORSE WEDDING CUVÉE
Salmon and Scallop Carpaccio
—124—

S. ANDERSON BRUT
Prawns with Champagne Butter
—126—

SCHRAMSBERG BLANC DE NOIRS
Sea Bass in Parchment with Leeks and Ginger
—128—

SCHRAMSBERG BRUT ROSÉ (CUVÉE DE PINOT)
Mushroom Tart
—130—

SCHRAMSBERG CRÉMANT
Nectarine Tart
—132—

PINOT NOIR 🍇 134

ACACIA PINOT NOIR, RESERVE CARNEROS
Grilled Small Birds
—136—

AU BON CLIMAT PINOT NOIR, SANFORD & BENEDICT
Roast Prime Rib with Au Gratin Potatoes
—138—

CALERA PINOT NOIR, JENSEN
Squab Salad with Sherry Vinegar and Red Wine Sauce
—140—

ROBERT MONDAVI WINERY PINOT NOIR, RESERVE
Sautéed Duck Breasts with Olive and Caper Sauce
—142—

SANFORD PINOT NOIR
Roasted Vegetables Fettuccine
—144—

STONESTREET PINOT NOIR
Pan Fried Sea Scallops with Sautéed Leeks, Pinot Noir Sauce and Spicy Sugar Snap Peas
—146—

TALLEY VINEYARDS PINOT NOIR
Roasted Rack of Lamb with Pinot Noir Sauce
—148—

WILD HORSE PINOT NOIR
Warm Mushroom Salad with Raspberry Vinaigrette
—150—

SYRAH/PETITE SIRAH 🍇 152

BONNY DOON LE CIGARE VOLANT
Veal Chops with Blood Orange, Sage and Guajillo Sauce, Purple Mashed Potatoes, Sweet Creamed Spinach and Grilled Green Onions
—154—

KARLY (NOTSO) PETITE SIRAH
Kung Pao Lamb
—158—

THE OJAI VINEYARD SYRAH
Spicy Boneless Pork Loin Roast
—160—

QUPÉ SYRAH, BIEN NACIDO RESERVE
Grilled Lamb Chops with Sautéed Root Vegetables
—162—

STAG'S LEAP WINE CELLARS PETITE SIRAH
Savory Goat Cheese and Roasted Red Pepper Tart with Rosemary
—164—

ZINFANDEL 🍇 168

CAYMUS VINEYARDS ZINFANDEL
Cassoulet of Lentils Vertes du Puy with Lamb, Sausage and Pork
—170—

GRGICH HILLS ZINFANDEL
Chicken with Pine Nuts
—172—

NALLE WINERY ZINFANDEL
Venison Steaks with Zinfandel, Chipotle Roasted Shallots and Pecan Sauce
—174—

RIDGE ZINFANDEL, LYTTON SPRINGS
Game with Mexican Cocoa, Zinfandel and Black Chile Sauce
—176—

STORYBOOK MOUNTAIN VINEYARDS ZINFANDEL
Le Chapeau du Cochon Storybook
—178—

CABERNET SAUVIGNON 180

CAKEBREAD CELLARS CABERNET SAUVIGNON
Venison Stew with Dried Cherries
—184—

CARMENET MERITAGE, MOON MOUNTAIN
Braised Beef Short Ribs
—186—

CAYMUS VINEYARDS CABERNET SAUVIGNON
RCK Raspberry Barbecued Lamb
—188—

CAYMUS VINEYARDS CABERNET SAUVIGNON,
SPECIAL SELECTION
Grilled Filet of Beef with Parsnip Mashed Potatoes
—190—

CHATEAU MONTELENA CABERNET SAUVIGNON
Venison Chops Montelena
—192—

DIAMOND CREEK CABERNET SAUVIGNON,
RED ROCK TERRACE
Filet Mignon with Portobello Mushroom Sauce, Julienned
Vegetables and Potato Cake with Roasted Tomato
—194—

DUCKHORN VINEYARDS HOWELL MOUNTAIN RED
Filet Mignon Finale
—196—

DUCKHORN VINEYARDS MERLOT
Grilled Wild Duck with Ducky's Wild Duck Port Sauce
—198—

FISHER VINEYARDS CABERNET SAUVIGNON, COACH INSIGNIA
Picnic Lamb Kabobs
—200—

GIRARD WINERY CABERNET SAUVIGNON
Mignon of Game with Persimmon Sauce
—202—

GRGICH HILLS CABERNET SAUVIGNON
Pan-roasted Ribeye Steak with Wine Sauce
—204—

HEITZ CELLAR CABERNET SAUVIGNON,
MARTHA'S VINEYARD
Veal Luisa
—206—

JORDAN CABERNET SAUVIGNON
Marinated California Goat Cheese
—208—

MARTIN BROS. WINERY CABERNET ETRUSCO
New York Steaks with Wild Mushroom Ragout
—210—

LOUIS M. MARTINI CABERNET SAUVIGNON, RESERVE
Spaghettini Primavera
—212—

MAYACAMAS VINEYARDS CABERNET SAUVIGNON
Beef Tenderloin
—214—

OPUS ONE
Grilled Lamb with Black Currants
—216—

RIDGE CABERNET SAUVIGNON, MONTE BELLO
Peppered Roast Lamb Loin with Vegetable Panache
—220—

ROBERT MONDAVI WINERY
CABERNET SAUVIGNON, RESERVE
Veal Chops Chasseur
—224—

ROBERT PECOTA CABERNET SAUVIGNON, KARA'S VINEYARD
Flank Steak Marinade
—226—

ROBERT PECOTA MERLOT, STEVEN ANDRE VINEYARD
Grilled Leg of Lamb Pecota
—228—

SIMI WINERY CABERNET SAUVIGNON
Black Olive Pesto Pizette
—230—

SPOTTSWOODE CABERNET SAUVIGNON
Polenta E Ragu Di Selvaggina
(Polenta with Rabbit and Game Birds Stew)
—232—

STAG'S LEAP WINE CELLARS CABERNET SAUVIGNON, FAY
Herb-Cured Filet of Beef with Horseradish Sauce
—234—

STAG'S LEAP WINE CELLARS CABERNET SAUVIGNON, S.L.V.
Roast Rack of Lamb with Grilled Polenta,
Cabernet Sauce and Seared Vegetables
—236—

STAGLIN FAMILY VINEYARD CABERNET SAUVIGNON
Grilled Veal Chop with Grainy Mustard Marinade
—240—

TREFETHEN CABERNET SAUVIGNON
Grilled Pork Tenderloin with Thyme-Infused Cabernet Sauce
—242—

DESSERT 🍇 244

HEITZ CELLAR ANGELICA
Tiramisu
—245—

LOUIS M. MARTINI MOSCATO AMABILE
Amiably Sliced Pears
—248—

ROBERT PECOTA MOSCATO D'ANDREA
Zabaglione and Marinated Fresh Fruit
—250—

FOREWORD

*W*INE IS ELEGANCE. Whether the golden straw color of whites or deep-purple reds, whether packaged in stoutish clear broad shoulders or green-tinted long-necked bottles, when fine wine is poured into stemmed crystal it creates a mood, a style, of deep appreciation for the art that created it. Truly, a well-crafted wine is like any work of art: It so testifies when swirled in a glass, releasing its aromas; it so testifies when tasted, expressing its many flavors; it so testifies as it lingers in aftertaste, stamping its qualities into your memory.

*W*INE IS ROMANCE. The love of the land and its bounty, as reflected in the winemaker's efforts to produce each bottle, translating these gifts from the earth into liquid celebrations of life. The love for the taste that each grape, each wine, distinctly provides, and with it the adventure and the passion that makes each wine special. The love from sharing this feeling with friends, with lovers, and the warmth and comfort that is inherent with each opportunity.

*W*INE IS HEALTH. From its capabilities to slightly thin the blood, to its contribution to good times and good feelings, a lightening of the spirit and a reverence for life, wine makes for physical, mental and spiritual well-being. We toast to a good life, and that is what wine can bring.

That wine can also be none of the above is not the fault of wine, but of how it is perceived and misused; that is the danger of alcohol and its abusers. But when the three facets above are desired, embraced and honored intelligently, then wine is elevated to a standard that makes for an embellished existence on earth. It is to that standard which this book aspires.

"Now that we have the wine, what are we going to eat?" For some, posing this question is like the tail wagging the dog. On many occasions, after tasting a luscious Kistler Chardonnay or a gloriously berry-laden Nalle Zinfandel, have you asked, "Wouldn't this go great with (blank)?" This book will help you fill in that blank.

So where did this book come from?

Actually, it came about quite fortuitously. In the fall of 1992, as we were barbecueing next to each other at a UCLA football game (wine bottles on casual display), we struck up a conversation and quickly found ourselves sharing a mutual dream of a wine-food book. We shook hands and became partners on the spot.

We believed it was important to create a cookbook that stressed wine first, featuring bottles of fine wine matched with gourmet recipes to enhance them. We then concentrated on only those top-ranked California wineries that offered quality varietals with consistent characteristics, so that no matter what vintage used the recipe would be correct. The participating wineries supplied the wines and most of the recipes as well. In some cases leading restaurants provided recipes or we came up with a few of our own.

The fun and challenging experience was in personally testing each wine with its companion recipe. We used a "normal" household kitchen using supplies readily available at nearby retail stores. Thus the ease of preparation for the average household was ensured. So, from abalone to zabaglione, these recipes work, as our notes attest.

When it comes to matching wine with food, it's usually wise to follow the tried-and-true Rule:

Whites go with white meat,

Reds go with red meat.

Its explication makes perfect sense. White wines tend to be more delicate and subtle, as do fish and fowl, while reds are bolder and more assertive, able to hold their own with thick-flavored roasts and steaks. Exceptions to this rule don't make it wrong nor even weaken it—it's just acceptable as the simple norm.

Within this two-part construct are basic subdivisions: For whites, Sauvignon Blancs and their more crispy cousins lend themselves well to mollusks and light-flavored fish; Chardonnays, usually more deeply accented wines, favorably match up with meaty fish and all fowl; and the saucy Germans love to do friendly battle with rich and spicy foods of any origin. As for the reds, it's more general and, iron-ically, individual—the softer the flavor in the wine (some Pinot Noirs and Merlots), the softer its culinary counterparts should be; the more aggressive the flavor, the broader food flavor strokes it can handle (again some Pinot Noirs, Cabernet Sauvignons and Bordeaux, even Zinfandels and Syrahs). Therefore, with reds it's more how the meat is prepared than what kind it is.

As implied earlier, there can be reasons to ignore this simplistic sys-tem, and several examples in this book do just that. But "The Rule" exists because it works, as most maxims do.

There are two other aspects to the wine-as-food concept: serving temperature and breathing. Whites are chilled, reds are served at room temperature or slightly below (the slightly-chilled Beaujolais a notable exception). However, when it comes to putting a chill on a white wine, too much cold literally masks flavors or makes them dis-appear altogether, flavors that can then only emerge when the intense chill wears off.

Breathing is intended to "open up" a wine, acclimating it to the world outside its cramped environment, and thereby allowing it to re-lease its restrained qualities. This might best be accomplished by de-canting the wine a short while before serving. Some contend that roughly pouring a wine into a decanter, thereby aerating the liquid, speeds this process considerably; others feel this can maltreat a wine and potentially subvert it. With certain well-aged wines that will def-initely occur. Some think the entire concept of officially breathing a wine, whether uncorking the bottle an hour or two beforehand or de-canting, is pretentious bunk. Be that as it may, wine does change its character once it is poured, different flavors can come and go as the wine reacts to air.

Now, armed as you are with this knowledge, we suggest you make note of those qualities in the wines you taste that compare with the following wines. Find as many excuses as you can to invite friends over and put this book to excellent use.

We have!

—HENDRIK VAN LEUVEN & RON BREITSTEIN

INTRODUCTION

Jack Davies, Owner
Schramsberg Vineyards and Cellars

*C*ONTINUED MEDICAL RESEARCH has brought us more and more good news about the healthful benefits of wine—when consumed in moderation. In many ways all of this is not really new. The enjoyment of wine and noting its positive effects goes far back in the recorded history of humanity.

The diversity of wine is one of the most outstanding aspects of its appeal. The notion that there could be such a thing as the "perfect" Cabernet or Chardonnay overlooks the simple fact that not everyone's taste is the same. Newcomers to wine certainly don't bring the same taste perceptions as some hard core, long time wine drinkers—and even they can find some ways to disagree on the merits of any wine.

That's where personal preference steps in, and thank goodness for it! A rich, tannic, aged Cabernet might well appeal to a professional wine writer and earn 98 points on his or her rating system, but to the palate of an equally experienced taster who prefers a softer or fresher or fruitier style, that 98 might seem too generous. Thankfully for all of us, they're both right. And it's easy to see why, because wine is so complicated to make.

Wine production is an incredible road to travel. The many varieties of grapes are not at all the same, and the vineyards in which they are grown can be worlds apart in their soil or particular climatic conditions. Just these two circumstances of grape and soil can produce enormous variety in aroma, flavor and body in the wines they produce.

Then as the winemakers approach the fruit they can create unbelievable variation in the final result. One winemaker may decide to ferment in a refrigerated stainless steel tank to retain maximum natural freshness from the grape juice. Another might decide to ferment the juice in oak barrels (used or new) and thus introduce distinct flavors and aromas from the wood. He might decide to introduce the softer lactic acid and change the volume of the sharper malic acid originally present, which will have a profound effect on the flavor and texture of the wine. He could stick to one sequence of this process every year, or could separately do any combination of these things to a single crush and then produce a wide-range of effects from the same base wine which might appeal to many different tastes.

That's not all! There is aging, both in the barrel and in the bottle: How long to age the wine before bottling? How long after being bottled before releasing? Both judgments can create wonderful character variation which may appeal more to some than to others.

Finally, you the wine drinker become a part of this process too. How long should you let a bottle age before opening it? Every wine changes, sometimes subtly, sometimes dramatically, depending on how it's stored and for how long. It's a wonderful guessing game, and it allows you to be the ultimate judge.

Perhaps most important to remember is that wine is food, and is meant to be consumed as such. This book is a large step in validating that concept, approaching wine as food first, and finding those dishes, those meals, to suit each bottle best.

Explore this diversity with your food. Try two totally different Cabernets with a meal, side by side, and talk about them with your friends. Or choose three vintages of the same wine from the same producer, and compare each of them with your meal. You'll find it exciting, appealing and revealing. Keep going—try some of the less-common grape varieties with your dining—Pinot Blanc, Gewürztraminer, Syrah, and dozens more. You will find that many of these wines are more attractive with a particular food than you might have thought.

And there is also the world of sparkling wine. Don't think they are just bubbles, please. Realize that behind those drinkable stars can be the same effort in choice of grapes, method of fermentation, style of blending and age judgments. You will discover some remarkable wines from under those caged corks that can be just as appealing with a meal as any still wine.

So don't let anyone scare you away from your own appreciation. Don't be turned off by someone's "score" or opinion. If you like the wine, you're right—it's your judgment that matters! Which wine appeals to you with chicken or sole may not add the same dimension for you when drunk with pasta or a meat course. And what you enjoy with a particular dessert may not be someone else's first pick. No matter. The only person you need to please is you!

SAUVIGNON BLANC

*S*AUVIGNON BLANC is a dry white wine. Its spectrum of flavors ranges from herby-grassy to tartly fruity, and boasts a bright, distinctive and cleansing taste that matches supremely with mollusks, delicate seafood, and most shellfish. Originally from the Sauternes region of Bordeaux, fine French examples also come from Graves and the Loire Valley areas. It's most often released in a high-shouldered bottle, like its Bordeaux counterpart Cabernet Sauvignon. It is frequently blended with Semillon, usually to soften its acidity.

The Sauvignon Blanc varietal was first introduced into California in 1878 via cuttings from the premier French producer of Sauternes—Château d'Yquem—to the Wente Bros. in Livermore, which in turn provided cuttings for an astounding number of plantings throughout the state since. In fact, when the owner-son of the man who had provided the original cuttings from the Château tasted seven consecutive vintages produced at Wente, he wrote, "I am glad to find my children doing so well in California."

In the 1960s, Robert Mondavi was attempting to develop consumer interest in this varietal, but guessed that there might be some confusion within the burgeoning and under-educated wine-buying public between two wines bearing the Sauvignon name. In the Pouilly-sur-Loire region of France the Sauvignon Blanc is called Blanc-Fumé (or "smoked white," due to the grayish-bloom that covers the ripening berries). In an attempt to nomenclaturally separate this wine from its red counterpart, Mondavi more or less borrowed it, transposed the two words, and the "Fumé Blanc" was born. As such, it is strictly a California creation, and except for some relatively minor aspects (or claims thereof), the Sauvignon Blanc and the Fumé Blanc are one and the same varietal.

The best Sauvignon Blancs are diverse, complex wonders that can almost dance on the palate. In style, some can be crafted with vanilla-bearing oak and shaped to include hints of bell pepper and new-mown alfalfa, or they might be fruit-focused to reveal sprays of lemon grass and crisp Granny Smiths. Therein lies part of the rub: the nuances and interior pleasures of Sauvignon Blanc,

wine experts agree, take more pa-
tience to detect and discern. By the
same token, Sauvignon Blanc can be
a clean, refreshing splash of flavor
when served on its own, handles
hors d'oeuvres and cheese with great
panache, harmonizes with green salads wonderfully well, and can be as-
toundingly revealed with entrees of
great subtlety, delicacy and finesse.

Enjoying a fine Sauvignon Blanc
is almost like being in an exclusive
club whose members take gleeful
pride in surprising the unaware with
such rarities. Without a doubt, great
wine drinking experiences await
those who are fortunate to be aware
of and enjoy the wines that follow,
and when paired with their suggested recipes may provide an even
more heightened satisfaction.

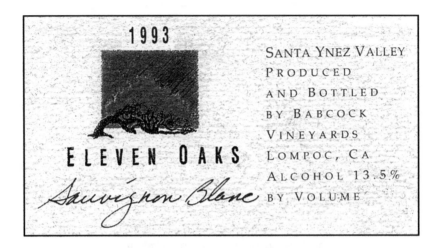

BABCOCK VINEYARDS SAUVIGNON BLANC
ELEVEN OAKS RANCH

...is warmly golden in color, with rich, excellently balanced fruit and herbaceousness in the nose, simply exploding with classy Sauvignon Blanc character. It has full body weight in the mouth, rich, almost creamy. Delicious traces of grassiness along with the grand doses of fruit. Smooth, enjoyable, a great drinking wine.

SERVE WITH
TAGLIATELLE WITH GRILLED CHICKEN BREAST, PANCETTA AND ROSEMARY GREMOLATA

This recipe combines several remarkable elements to create a complete pasta-based meal. Tagliatelle pasta (in a pinch, substitute fettuccini) is available at most Italian delis where you can find the Italian pancetta bacon as well, although Canadian will suffice, and if you can somehow find bacon that has been applewood smoked, you've hit on the original recipe's request. The "gremolata" is an aromatic sprinkling of herbs and citrus zest that further accents the vegetables that abound throughout. This is a fantastic, all-in-one-course meal, a modified version of the proven winner at Walt's Wharf, the Babcock's restaurant in Seal Beach, California, as originally crafted by chef Hugh Leavitt. (4 servings)

MARINADE
1 cup balsamic vinegar
2 teaspoons minced garlic
1 teaspoon black pepper
1/2 teaspoon sea salt

INGREDIENTS
1 pound boneless, skinless
  chicken breasts
2 ounces olive oil
6 ounces bacon (Italian, Canadian,
  or other meaty "round"
  style—not American strips)
8 ounces red peppers—roasted,
  deseeded, and peeled, then

sliced into 1/4" x 2" strips
8 ounces asparagus tips
4 ounces Marsala wine
24 ounces beef stock
2 teaspoons sea salt
1 teaspoon ground black pepper
1 pound tagliatelle pasta
2 teaspoons rosemary gremolata:
  2 teaspoons each finely
  ground lemon and lime zest
  1 teaspoon each finely minced
  fresh rosemary and garlic
1/2 - 3/4 cup Parmesan cheese,
  freshly grated

1. Marinate chicken in marinade for 1-2 hours before cooking.
2. Grill on barbecue, then slice into 1/2" pieces.
3. In a large sauté pan, heat the oil. Add the chicken, bacon and peppers, and sauté briefly.
4. Deglaze the pan with the Marsala, then reduce 50%.
5. Add the stock, asparagus, salt and pepper. Reduce heat to a fast simmer.
6. Place the tagliatelle in boiling salted water and cook until three-quarters done. Drain the pasta and add it to the sauce (do not rinse the pasta, the starch will help give the sauce substance).
7. Simmer the pasta and sauce until the sauce has slightly thickened and reduced approximately 60%.
8. Place the pasta in a serving dish and sprinkle the gremolata evenly over the top.
9. Garnish with freshly grated Parmesan cheese and serve immediately.

THE WINE WITH THIS RECIPE

…has its fruit extracted even more. The pepper in the food elicits the complexities in the wine, and its smoothness is given an intriguing edge. The zest generates a wisp of citrus in the wine that otherwise may be hidden, and improves the finish. Great wine, great food, a great pairing!

BRANDER VINEYARD SAUVIGNON BLANC
Cuvée Nicolas

...has a rich, golden color, with a soft balance of herbaceousness and fruit in the nose, high-quality Sauvignon Blanc aromas. It provides a nice crispness in the mouth, well-constructed acid/fruit balance with a pleasing finish. A very tasty wine.

Serve with
Rotisserie Chicken Paulita

This recipe from Hendrik Van Leuven was inspired by two things: Hendrik's wife Paula, and our appreciation for this wine. Paula absolutely dotes on rotisserie chicken, recalling happy times back in her native Mexico; we simply dote on Brander Sauvignon Blanc, and were thrilled to find this works so well. The slow cooking the bell peppers receive, influenced by the chicken, makes their flavor unique and appropriate. Given the easy-going nature of the cooking process, this is a great way to spend an outdoor afternoon. (4 servings)

1 roaster chicken (3 1/2 - 4 1/2 lbs.)	1 tablespoon each fresh oregano,
4 cloves garlic, crushed	thyme, marjoram
1/2 cup balsamic vinegar	1/2 tablespoon red pepper
1/4 cup olive oil	Salt, fresh ground pepper
1/2 cup white wine	2 red bell peppers
1/4 cup lime juice	Corn tortillas, 2-3 per person

1. Combine all the ingredients except red bell peppers and tortillas, place in plastic bag, and marinate the chicken for 4-24 hours.

2. Prior to cooking, take red bell peppers, core, remove seeds and membranes, then slice into large wedges.

3. Stuff chicken cavity tightly with peppers, as many as you can squeeze in, then truss.

4. Slide in rotisserie skewer, and secure.

5. When barbecue fire has reached optimum level, separate it into two sections, leaving an open area below where the chicken will cook; place a foil "catch" pan for the juices, which can be used for gravy if desired (this indirect heat method is best for cooking any fowl on the 'cue).

6. Slow roast chicken over charcoals or mesquite until done (anywhere from $1^1/2$-3 hours, depending on lifestyle—the longer, the more thought-provoking). Add 3-7 briquets per fireside at the half-way point to maintain coals.

7. Remove chicken to carving platter.

8. While letting it cool a bit, heat tortillas two-at-a-time on a small skillet, heating each side until just hot, flipping both over then flipping the now-hot tortilla over on its cooking counterpart. Continue heating and "shuffling" tortillas until all four sides have been thoroughly heated. (Two to three pans working at once can be quite exhilarating; sure, you can use tongs, but fast fingers are much more inspiring!)

9. Wrap heated tortillas in a towel to keep warm, and place them in a covered container or tortilla warmer

10. Serve sliced portions or sections of chicken and cooked peppers with the hot tortillas.

THE WINE WITH THIS RECIPE

...becomes richer and more full-bodied. The herbaceousness jumps out a little more in the palate, and the wine develops a more elegant finish. The peppers, basted by the chicken juices, become a tangy accompaniment with the oak in the wine, and the chicken itself with its marinade pulls the fruit out more. A most enjoyable and satisfying combination.

Cakebread Cellars

NAPA VALLEY

Sauvignon Blanc

1993

PRODUCED AND BOTTLED BY CAKEBREAD CELLARS
RUTHERFORD, CALIFORNIA, USA
ALCOHOL 14.1% BY VOLUME

CAKEBREAD CELLARS SAUVIGNON BLANC

…has a light, golden color, with distinct fruit flavors, good body, and a long, nice, lingering finish. Good and dry, full and satisfying in the mouth, a nice richness for a Sauvignon Blanc. Balanced, not overly grassy or herbaceous; takes a while to open up, but is enhanced when allowed to do so.

SERVE WITH
STEAMED MUSSELS WITH GARLIC AND WHITE WINE

Fresh mussels are of the essence, and will provide thoughts of seaside luxuries with little preparation. The mussels, the broth their liquid and the wine produce, the hard-shell French bread, and a tossed green salad, are all you need for a great and casual summer meal. This enjoyable recipe is the product of the winery's Resident Chef Brian Streeter and Dolores Cakebread. (4 servings)

6 pounds mussels—choose ones that are large and feel heavy
1/4 cup extra virgin olive oil
2 tablespoons shallots, minced
1 tablespoon garlic, minced
2 tablespoons parsley, flat leaf, minced
1 cup dry white wine (Sauvignon Blanc)
1 loaf crusty French bread

1. Scrub the mussels and remove the beard that is attached between the shells; pull hard, and try to remove all the hair. Discard any mussels that don't close after being tapped.
2. In a pot large enough to hold all the mussels, sauté garlic and shallots in the olive oil to soften.
3. Add the wine, parsley and mussels. Bring to a boil, cover, and steam until mussels open, about 5-9 minutes; shake the pan occasionally like a popcorn pan, to shift the shells and encourage the cooking. After a point, watch to see that they don't cook too long, as mussels will lose their plumpness and become tough. Some of the meat may be salmon-red, others white—both are perfectly normal.
4. Serve in large bowls with plenty of the broth, along with the French bread to soak up the garlic broth.

THE WINE WITH THIS RECIPE
...finds its acids working in concert with the seafood. All of the positive qualities of this wine are enhanced by the rusticity of the meal. The richness of its balanced grassy-herbaceousness is elevated by the parsley and garlic in the mussel-infused broth. This casual meal gains stature with this pairing.

MERITAGE
1993

armenet

PARAGON VINEYARD
SAUVIGNON BLANC 70%
SEMILLON 30%
EDNA VALLEY

CARMENET MERITAGE
PARAGON VINEYARD

...features an inviting golden color, with an opulent, fruity nose, full of attractive herbaceousness, a bit of floral perfume from the Semillon and is softly oaky. It provides an engagingly dry feel in the mouth, with wonderful balance, as its blend of pear, fruit and just a hint of citrus glide through the soft creaminess, winding up to a gentle, caressing finish.

SERVE WITH
PASTINA RISOTTO WITH CRISPY ROCK SHRIMP AND SPICY ROASTED PEPPER PURÉE

Master Napa Valley chef Michael Chiarello of Tra Vigne Restaurant created this twist on pasta, with dashes and flashes of spice and capsicum to heighten the effect. The pasta is actually cooked in two stages in order for it to emerge risotto-like without the lengthy process (and which can be prepared in advance without loss of quality). You can adjust the zip in the pepper purée by choosing between the jalepeño and the slightly-less-picante serrano peppers, or to obtain only a slight sense of such heat simply replace one of the red peppers with a poblano prepared in the same fashion and omit the smaller devil; as this makes at least a full cup, there will be plenty left over for use as a salsa in other imaginative ways! (4 servings)

12 tablespoons spicy pepper purée
    4 red bell peppers, roasted, peeled and seeded
    1 jalapeño or serrano pepper, roasted, peeled and seeded
1 pound pastina (#78 Acini di

Pepe or other small "star" pasta)
5 tablespoons virgin olive oil
2 tablespoons chopped garlic
Salt and freshly ground pepper, to taste
2 tablespoons fresh chopped thyme

3 cups chicken stock (or low-salt chicken or vegetable broth)
4-6 cups peanut oil (or other natural flavored oil)
3/4 cup all-purpose flour
3/4 cup semolina flour
1 teaspoon salt
1/2 teaspoon pepper
1 1/2 pounds rock shrimp
1/2 cup buttermilk
1 cup grated Parmesan cheese
4 tablespoons butter (optional)

1. Purée the peppers until smooth, set aside.
2. Bring a large pot of salted water to a boil. Add the pastina and cook until it is slightly undercooked, about 11 minutes, stirring occasionally to prevent the pasta from sticking to the pan bottom. Drain the pasta, then place in ice water to retard further cooking; drain again and reserve.
3. Heat the olive oil in a saucepan over medium-high heat until hot. Add garlic and cook until light brown, moving pan on and off heat as necessary to regulate temperature. Add thyme—it should make a crackling sound as it hits the hot pan, like mini-firecrackers. Add the stock, raise to high heat, bring to a boil and reduce by half. (The pasta and stock reduction can be prepared in advance and assembled shortly before serving.)
4. While bringing the peanut oil to high frying heat, whisk the two flours together with the salt and pepper. Lightly coat the shrimp in the buttermilk and drain. Dredge the shrimp in the flour mixture, shake off the excess and cook in the hot oil for 1-2 minutes or until golden brown. Drain the shrimp on paper towels.
5. Add the cooked pastina to the reduced stock and return to a boil. Stir in the Parmesan and spicy pepper purée, then season with salt and pepper to taste. Swirl in butter, if desired, for an even richer-tasting dish.
6. Pour the pastina into a heated serving bowl or individual soup plates, top with crispy rock shrimp and serve.

THE WINE WITH THIS RECIPE

…increases in richness, as the slight spiciness of the peppers brightens the flavors and roundly intensifies the beauty of the herbaceousness. The oak becomes more pronounced, and the wine becomes more complete and intriguing overall, as it wends its way through the contributions from the cheese and the shrimp. This pairing helps define the meaning of wine and food complement.

DUCKHORN VINEYARDS

1994
NAPA VALLEY
SAUVIGNON BLANC

DUCKHORN VINEYARDS SAUVIGNON BLANC

...is light, golden straw in color, with a multifarious nose expressing good herbaceousness, citrus in the background, a glimpse of vanilla, crispness. Lots of fruit up front, medium-light body weight, attractive and pleasing, a lovely hint of lemon/citrus, a crisp and enormously drinkable wine.

SERVE WITH
SMOKED SALMON CHEESECAKE
WITH GREEN ONION COULIS

This wonderful, savory cheesecake was tailor-made to accompany this wine by Emeril Lagasse of Emeril's Restaurant in Napa Valley. It is certainly luscious, complex—and sure to cause a sensation. (8 servings)

1 cup freshly grated Parmesan cheese
1 cup bread crumbs
$1/2$ cup unsalted butter, melted
1 tablespoon olive oil
1 cup onions, chopped
$1/2$ cup chopped green bell peppers
$1/2$ cup chopped red bell peppers
2 teaspoons salt
12 turns freshly ground black pepper
$1^3/4$ pounds cream cheese, at room temperature
4 eggs

$1/2$ cup heavy cream
1 cup grated smoked Gouda cheese
1 pound (approx. 2 cups) smoked salmon, chopped
$2^1/4$ cups Green Onion Coulis:
  $3/4$ cup chopped green onions
  $1/2$ cup fresh parsley sprigs
  1 tablespoon chopped shallots
  1 tablespoon chopped garlic
  2 large eggs, at room temperature
  1 teaspoon salt
  6 turns freshly ground black pepper
  $1^1/2$ cups extra virgin olive oil

To prepare cheesecake

1. Preheat oven to 350°F.
2. Process the Parmesan cheese, bread crumbs, and butter until thoroughly blended, and press the mixture into the bottom and slightly up the sides of a 9" springform pan.
3. Heat the oil in a medium skillet over high heat. Add the onions, the green and red peppers, and sauté for 2 minutes, stirring and shaking the skillet to keep the ingredients moving.
4. Stir in the salt and pepper, sauté for 1 minute more, remove from the heat, and let cool.
5. Using an electric mixer, beat the cream cheese with the eggs in a large bowl until thick and frothy, about 4 minutes.
6. Beat in the cream, Gouda, sautéed vegetables, and the smoked salmon, and beat thoroughly until incorporated and creamy, for about 2 minutes.
7. Pour the filling into the prepared springform pan and bake until firm, about 1 1/4 hours.
8. Allow to cool to room temperature; if you refrigerate the cheesecake, also return to room temperature before serving, about 1 hour.

To prepare the Coulis

1. Place the green onions, parsley, shallots, and garlic in a food processor or blender and purée.
2. Add the eggs, salt and pepper, and continue to process.
3. With the machine running, slowly stream in the olive oil until it's thoroughly incorporated; it should achieve the consistency of mayonnaise.

To serve

Cut the cheesecake into wedges with a warm knife and serve each slice with 2-3 tablespoons of the freshly-made Green Onion Coulis.

The wine with this recipe

…gains a roundness, as the fruit meshes with the cheesecake and is elevated. The richness in the food makes this crisp wine improve. The delicacy of flavor from the smoked qualities in the salmon and Gouda has an extremely beneficial reaction to the herbaceousness in the wine. A lovely, very rich coupling.

FROG'S LEAP

1994 SAUVIGNON BLANC
NAPA VALLEY

PRODUCED & BOTTLED BY FROG'S LEAP, RUTHERFORD, CA

FROG'S LEAP SAUVIGNON BLANC

…is straw-golden in color, crisp smells of fruit, herbaceousness, citrus in nose. In the mouth, it's nice and crisp, good acid balance with the fruit, and its finish carries on the themes in the wine. Clearly a classic, lively and delicious Sauvignon Blanc.

SERVE WITH
PRAWN BARBECUE

This is a grilled favorite at Frog's Leap, originally created by Julie Williams, co-owner of the winery. Served either as a first course at outdoor gatherings or as a main entree accompanied by rice and grilled tomato halves, the marinade calls for fresh herbs and a variance of red pepper flakes (depending on your Scovill tolerances). It's cooked in-shell, a method that has long been understood to add a wonderful "seaness" to the flavor, and served in-shell, so diners peel the shell off themselves—truly fabulous finger-food that requires ample napkins and perhaps a few water-damp towels! (4 servings)

1 pound medium-to-large prawns
   (approximately 4 or more per person, unshelled)
3 tablespoons extra-virgin olive oil
3 cloves fresh garlic, crushed
$1/2$ cup dill or basil (or other favorite garden herb), minced
1-2 teaspoons red pepper flakes
1 teaspoon fresh ground sea salt
Fresh ground pepper, to taste
$1/4$ cup white wine (Frog's Leap Sauvignon Blanc)
Fresh sourdough, French, or herb bread loaf
Lemon wedges

FOR THE MARINADE
30-60 minutes ahead of serving, lightly rinse the prawns, drain, and place in plastic bag. Toss with oil; add crushed garlic, pepper flakes (to nerve), minced herbs, sea salt and pepper. Seal and refrigerate. 10 minutes prior to cooking, add wine, and mix thoroughly.

TO COOK
With grill coals sharply hot, place the prawns on the grill; turn quickly as the shells change to a bright pink color. Serve in a warm, shallow communal bowl garnished with sprigs of the herbs. Serve with savory bread and lemon wedges.

THE WINE WITH THIS RECIPE
...enjoys its encounter. The lightness in both match up well, with the wine becoming a touch more sweet, its wood gracefully emerging from the garlic. With the spiciness of the pepper bouncing off the crispness of the wine, the dill becomes deliciously evident with the wine's herbaceousness. A quiet, flavorful combination of elements.

GRGICH HILLS FUMÉ BLANC

...is light-medium gold in color, with exciting fruit and herbaceousness along with touches of vanilla-oak and pear, a most attractive nose. Medium-full in the mouth, the herbaceousness is pleasingly prevalent, along with slight grapefruit-citrus flavors. With good balance of fruit and oak, attractive richness, this is a wine with style and class.

SERVE WITH
AHI CARPACCIO SALAD

This simple-to-construct recipe comes from world-famous Michael's Restaurant in Santa Monica, California. However, the challenge comes in its being a sushi-like raw fish dish, and there is the added wrinkle of the desired fresh truffles ("white" available only around November-December, "black" in December-March). There are jarred alternatives, but that's what they are, alternatives. With the level of excellence that is the mark of a fine restaurateur like Michael McCarty, if you're going to do it, do it right! (8 servings)

1 ahi filet, approximately 1 1/2 pounds
6 medium-size bunches arugula, stemmed, leaves separated
Salt and freshly ground black pepper
6 tablespoons fruity green extra virgin olive oil
6 ounces Parmesan cheese, freshly grated
1 ounce fresh black or white truffles
1 lemon, cut into 6 wedges

Chill the ahi in the refrigerator for 30-40 minutes, to firm it up for slicing. With a sharp knife, cut the ahi across the grain into 1/8" thick slices. Place the slices, sides touching, on large serving plates, covering each plate from its center to within 3/4" of the rim. Arrange the arugula leaves around each plate, surrounding the ahi. Season each serving with salt and pepper to taste. Drizzle with olive oil and sprinkle with Parmesan cheese. With a truffle shaver or swivel-bladed vegetable peeler, shave the truffle over each serving. Serve with lemon wedges.

THE WINE WITH THIS RECIPE
...*becomes even richer, smoother and fuller. The citrusy-flavor is drawn out by the sweetness of the ahi, making the wine more fruity and inviting. The fresh truffles are at home with the light herbaceousness of the wine, and the tannins in the arugula create a tasty backdrop for the wine's oak. This combination is a treat!*

LONG VINEYARDS SAUVIGNON BLANC

...features a medium-gold/straw color, and reveals full richness, lots of fruit with nice herbal character and a touch of oak, its round nose filling the senses. In the mouth, its lushness is astounding while still maintaining a sense of citrus crispness, acid and fruit balancing each other magnificently, the finish a con-clusion of length and strength. The use of Chardonnay in this outstanding Sauvignon Blanc is clever and successful. Altogether quite a sophisticated wine.

SERVE WITH
INVOLTINI DI PESCE SPADE E GAMBERI
(MARINATED SCAMPI AND SWORDFISH A LA PRIMI)

This delicate, delightful approach to the more hefty natures of shrimp and swordfish was created in the kitchen at the fine Italian restaurant of Piero Selvaggio in Los Angeles, Primi. The unusual use of radic-chio, fried just prior to serving, along with the thyme, green pepper and shallots in the sauce and marinade, adds a balancing flavor of the earth with the oceanic elements, and creates a unique meld. Serve with the equally unique and singular Long Sauvignon Blanc, and this becomes a meal without equal. (4 servings)

12 medium scampi/shrimp, shelled, cleaned	6 ounces dry Vermouth
3 shallots, chopped	1 tablespoon minced green pepper
1 lemon, juiced	4 ounces sweet butter
1 bunch thyme, chopped	Canola oil
Salt	1 radicchio head, leaves rinsed and dried
9 ounces swordfish, dipped in milk	1 tomato, chopped

1. Place shrimp in a bowl with one of the chopped shallots, lemon juice, chopped thyme and a pinch of salt.
2. As the shrimp begins to marinate, cut the swordfish into thin slices, and then combine it with the shrimp, rolling it all together well, and refrigerate for 30 minutes.
3. Place the remaining shallot in a sauté pan, add the Vermouth and pepper, and simmer for three minutes on low heat.
4. Add the butter a dollop at a time, and mix with a whisk until the mixture finally becomes lightly creamy. Set aside for final preparation.
5. Cook the seafood mixture on a slightly oiled griddle for three minutes.
6. After which, flash fry the radicchio in a wok until just tender.
7. Make a bed of radicchio on each plate.
8. Place a quarter of the seafood on the radicchio and ladle on some sauce.
9. Top with the chopped tomatoes, and serve.

THE WINE WITH THIS RECIPE

…has a sudden brightness added to it. The fruit stands out, with the richness of the Chardonnay prevalent, along with the assured crispness of the Sauvignon Blanc. The shallots and pepper, with the slight bitterness of the radicchio, add to the herbaceousness, and the citrus in the wine blends magically with the fish. A major construction!

1994

NAPA VALLEY
TO-KALON VINEYARD

FUMÉ BLANC
RESERVE

UNFILTERED

ROBERT MONDAVI WINERY

ROBERT MONDAVI WINERY FUMÉ BLANC, RESERVE

...is straw-golden in color, and provides good herbaceousness in the nose, with hints of fruit and grass, faint oak, a full aroma. Excellent body feel in mouth, very smooth, full-bodied with great fruit and hint of oak. A substantial, creamy wine, with just enough tart and tang in the finish to give it a fresh lift.

SERVE WITH

SAVORY GOAT CHEESE CHEESECAKE

A delicious, rich and intriguingly flavorful lunch entree or appetizer, this can be served as is or modified in a number of ways to incorporate any vegetables you'd like to try within the cheese medium, such as red and green bell peppers or onions. The convenience of being able to make this in advance and refrigerate is a much appreciated bonus when it comes to entertaining—just allow enough time to return to room temperature before serving. This is a creation by Sarah Scott, Executive Chef at the Robert Mondavi Wine & Food Center in Orange County, California. (8 servings)

CRUST
3/4 cup bread crumbs
3/4 cup walnuts
3 tablespoons melted butter
FILLING
3/4 pound aged goat cheese (a decent Chevre or grated aged Tome)

1 1/4 pounds cream cheese, room temperature
4 eggs
1 clove garlic, crushed
1/4 teaspoon dried tarragon or 1 teaspoon fresh tarragon, chopped
Salt and pepper, to taste
1/4 cup whipping cream (about)

1. Place walnuts in food processor, pulse with metal blade until finely chopped.
2. Combine with bread crumbs, place on a baking sheet and lightly toast under the broiler—be careful not to let it burn.
3. Put crust mixture in processor and blend. Add butter, pulse until moistened and thoroughly combined.
4. Press into bottom and slightly up sides of an 8" springform pan.
5. In mixer, beat goat cheese and cream cheese to thoroughly combine. Add eggs, one at a time, beating well to incorporate.
6. Add garlic and tarragon, combine well.
7. Add cream, approximately 1/4 cup to thin the mixture—it should be the consistency of mayonnaise but not too liquidy. Taste for salt and pepper.
8. Pour filling into prepared springform pan. Bake at 350°F for 45-60 minutes, checking at 45 for doneness—it ultimately should be golden, puffed, and not loose in the center.
9. Remove from the oven, cool on rack in order to let it set up (it will collapse) for about 30 minutes before slicing. (May be refrigerated but should be served at room temperature.)

THE WINE WITH THIS RECIPE

…becomes richer tasting. The tartness and herbaceousness is subdued a bit, the oak is positively accented, and the smoothness matches up with the creaminess of the cake handsomely. The wine and recipe sublimely complement each other.

ROBERT PECOTA WINERY SAUVIGNON BLANC

…is of the classic herbaceous-grassy style, gloriously detectable in the nose. The touch of oak adds a luster to its taste of pear, with a smooth, creamy feel in the mouth, rounded and soft. As it approaches room temperature, even more mellowness emerges.

ZUCCHINI FRITATTA

A simple, country custard, employing the earthy flavor of zucchini highlighted by garlic, parsley, onion and Parmesan. A creation of Susan Pecota, this has proven to be a family favorite for many years, and is wonderful served warm or chilled. (4-6 servings)

1 pound zucchini (3-4 small)
1 yellow onion, chopped
2 tablespoons olive oil
4 eggs, lightly beaten
1/4 cup milk
2 cups Parmesan cheese (or more!)
2 tablespoons chopped parsley
1 clove garlic, minced
1 teaspoon each salt, fresh ground black pepper

1. Place zucchini into a pot of steaming water on a strainer, steam until just tender, then chop in a bowl.
2. Lightly sauté onion in olive oil until just brown.
3. Add onion and all other ingredients to zucchini. Pour into a lightly oiled baking dish and bake 1 hour at 350°F or until firm.

THE WINE WITH THIS RECIPE
…is superbly mated, accenting the vegetative qualities of the squash and onions to a fare-thee-well, and with the garlic and cheese it is a wondrous meal to savor and enjoy. A most refreshing way to celebrate the flavors of the earth!

SPOTTSWOODE SAUVIGNON BLANC

...*is medium-gold in color, with a full, rich Sauvignon Blanc nose—fruit, herbs, and a slight hint of fennel, deep aromas in all. It has full, rich, robust flavors along with a tremendous mouth feel. There is a glance of citrus, pleasing herbs, and an entirely seductive finish, as it holds up as long as possible. A most wonderful wine.*

Roasted Chilean Sea Bass
with Creamy Rock Shrimp Sauce

A fabulously easy recipe to make, with a touch of the dramatic thrown in via a moment of flambé. This was provided by Robert Simon of Pasadena, California's Bistro 45, via his chef, Hide Kurokawa, and has all the makings of a standard. (4 servings)

1 teaspoon garlic, chopped	3 ounces Florida rock shrimp
1 shallot, chopped	$1^1/2$ ounces brandy
2 teaspoons olive oil	1 tablespoon butter
6 ounces white wine	6 ounces Chilean sea bass
15 ounces fish stock	Tomato concasse (two chopped
6 ounces veal stock	fresh tomatoes)
6 ounces heavy cream	Chopped chives

1. Sauté garlic and shallot in olive oil in medium-sized sauce pot over medium heat until shallot begins to clear.
2. Add wine, reduce by half.
3. Add fish and veal stocks, and again reduce by half.
4. Add cream, and gently simmer until reduced by $2/3^{rds}$.
5. Sauté shrimp on high heat for 1 minute, reduce flame, add brandy and flambé. Add shrimp to sauce.
6. Rub medium sauté pan with butter, place sea bass in the center, then place pan in a 450°F oven for 6 minutes, or until fish is firm to the touch, remove.
7. Place a portion of the fish on each dinner plate, and add the sauce.
8. Garnish with tomato concasse and chopped chives, and serve.

The wine with this recipe
...has its richness accelerated. An intense combination, the sauce's profuse complexities find match after match within the wine, its fruitiness being given a fresh platform to work from. Even the chives are given a chance to make a statement with the herbaceousness in the wine. This wine is grown up.

CHARDONNAY

THE BEAUTIFUL THING about Chardonnay is that it is not only a great wine, but the most popular. Its demand has proved to be a boon to both wine growers and wine consumers: Wine growers depend on its continuing marketability to support their operations, and consumers benefit because the winemakers are continually working on pleasing their palates. That this wine lends itself to so many interpretations and flavor bases is another remarkable bonus, in that as varied as are the tastes that this wine can produce, so too are the recipes and meals that can be draped around them. It's no wonder that we are featuring so many Chardonnays in our book, because the majority of white wine drinkers enjoy it so much. To our minds, there's nothing wrong with being a favorite!

It's not an automatically easy grape to grow. It blooms early, making it vulnerable to spring frosts. Birds can be a problem, as the skins are thin, easily punctured, and unwanted pre-fermentation can take place. The delicate nature of the fruit means hand harvesting is best, the small short

clusters making it all the more difficult. Thankfully, its intense popular-
ity eases some of the financial strain
this entails.

Of white wine grapes, Chardonnay offers the winemaker perhaps
the most stylistic choices of all, each
decision capable of having an impact
on the end result. The list includes:
type of soil, elevation, sun/leaf/clus-
ter exposure, irrigation; time of day
(or night!) of harvest; the degree of
ripeness and its constituents, the
brix (sugar content), the pH and the
acid levels; crush technique, including skin and stem contact; stainless
steel fermentation and aging, or oak
aging in new or used ("old") barrels
or a combination of both, French
and/or American wood, how much
of the interior of the barrels should
be charred or "toasted," and the
length of time to be left in either; malo-lactic fermentation (a detailed ex-
planation of which follows); when to
bottle, whether to blend, whether to
filter and with what system, whether
to fine and with what substance to
use (isinglass, egg white, etc.), how
long to bottle age, and finally when
to release. The complexities of these
choices and many more are hard
enough without Mother Nature's
vagueries tossed in to really make
things difficult. Much praise is de-
served for those who are able to successfully navigate their way through

such shoals of winemaking.

Many California Chardonnays under-go a secondary fermentation, malo-lactic (or ML), in which the more tart malic acid naturally found in fermented wine is converted via a second bacteria-intro-duced fermentation into the softer, lush-er lactic acid most often associated with milk products; in most Chardonnays this creates the "buttery" feel in the mouth, and tends to accentuate the vanilla from the oak. On the other hand, some winer-ies feel the fruit that is present in the wine would not benefit from this trans-formation and choose to leave it in its original malic state. Then again, some winemakers choose to employ partial ML, converting percentages of the wine, depending on the end result desired. In a way, it's wonderful how California Chardonnay can come in so many deli-cious varieties.

To show how two neighbors in the Central Coast of California, in some ways using very similar if not the same grapes, can differ: Jim Clendenen, "The Mind Be-hind" Au Bon Climat, ages his Chardon-nay in two barrel stages, going from new and one-year-old barrels to four- and five-year-old barrels for varying lengths of time, while Bruno D'Alfonso, Sanford's winemaker, ages his reserve in only 100% new oak. Both produce consistent-ly superior, breath-taking wine, making them both right in what they do!

Chardonnay's French pedigree is clear-cut. It originally hails from the Burgundy district, and is thus commonly referred to as White Burgundy. Other areas famous for their Chardonnays are Maconnais, home of Pouilly Fuissé, and Yonne, where Chablis lies; in fact, only Chardonnay grapes may be used in French Chablis. Unfortunately, in the United States and in other countries of the world, Chablis became simply "white wine," capable of being whatever the winemaker in that country put in the bottle. Hence, the reliance in the U.S. to designate "Chardonnay" as that wine that holds a true Burgundian heritage.

Chardonnay holds a special place in the development of the California wine industry during its drive to be regarded as world-class. It was at the momentous Bicentennial Tasting held in Paris, 1976, when Napa's Chateau Montelena 1973 Chardonnay took the honors at the blind tasting challenge from the two top French white Burgundy producers. This, along with Stag's Leap Wine Cellars' similar Cabernet Sauvignon victory over its Bordeaux counterparts, focused global attention on Napa, on California, and the floodgates were opened.

Certainly, Chardonnay is a tremendous varietal. Whether lean, austere and crisp, or lush, full-bodied and pliant, or anywhere in-between, it provides lasting enjoyment, especially with food. It well defines what this book attempts to do, as the following wines and recipes can delightfully attest.

ACACIA CHARDONNAY
RESERVE CARNEROS

…features an enticing medium-gold-to-straw color, with a nose of slight citrus and oak, an attractive and elegant roundness of flavors. It provides a satisfying richness in the mouth, with well-stamped Chardonnay flavors along with its touch of citrus, delightfully complex. There is just a hint of acid to give it an attractive bite, making it a truly elegant wine that flows easily through the senses and compels satisfaction.

SERVE WITH
VEAL STEW WITH FRESH HERBS

A thankfully uncomplicated way in which to feature veal with this remarkable white wine, one of the few crossover recipes to be featured. A creation of Susan Brooks, wife of winemaker Larry, this blending of vegetables and veal proves to be an absolute knockout combined with their wine. The vegetable amounts are varied, depending on amount of veal used; if you want a thicker-sauced stew, increase the flour at the #2 stage. Because this is a stew, veal shank can be used instead of loins with great success, although this increases the necessity of trimming undesired elements. (6 servings)

3-4 lbs. veal, cut into 1" pieces	3-4 cups carrots, chopped
1/4 pound butter	3-4 cups onions, chopped
1/2 cup flour	2-4 tablespoons fresh tarragon or dill
1 teaspoon nutmeg	3-4 cups chicken stock
Salt, pepper	1/2 -1 cup cream

1. Melt half the butter at moderate heat, and gently cook the meat—do not sear.
2. Add half the flour, the salt, pepper and nutmeg, and stir to combine.
3. Lower the heat slightly, and add the vegetables and continue cooking for 5 minutes.
4. Add half the herbs, then enough stock to cover the meat. Cover and simmer for 1 1/2 hours.
5. Strain the solids from the liquid, and save both.
6. Melt the second half of the butter in the same pot, and mix in the remaining flour to create a roux; cook over low heat for 5 minutes.
7. Mix the reserved liquid into the roux and simmer another 5 minutes.
8. Mix in the cream and the second portion of the herbs; return the reserved meat and vegetables to the pot, and simmer until heated through. Correct for salt and pepper, and serve.

THE WINE WITH THIS RECIPE

...has its creaminess opened like a blossom, an element present to begin with but cleverly enhanced by the coaxing from the stew's well-crafted qualities. The tarragon adds a pleasant sweetness not only to the wine but to the veal, creating an absolutely delicate thrust that blends their flavors enchantingly. It's an engagingly ambiguous combination—there's a constant wafting between being lush and being crisp that lets both approaches have its turn in the mouth with great success. It's a multi-dimensional match that works beautifully.

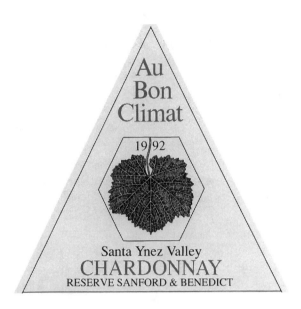

AU BON CLIMAT CHARDONNAY
SANFORD & BENEDICT

…displays a medium-golden color, rich in appearance, and offers luscious oak tones and expressions of fruit in the nose, outstanding fullness heralding great things to come. The taste brings pears and mild, attractive citrus to bear, the fruit mingling in the mouth with the deftly-crafted oak-borne vanilla influence, attractively robust bursts of flavors. Completed as it is by a gloriously persistent finish, this is truly a classic "White Burgundy" experience.

SERVE WITH
LOBSTER WITH SAFFRON RISOTTO

Risotto, the Italian rice specialty, gets an extra boost from a dash of saffron to go along with the lobster in this recipe specially created for this wine by Donna Oken, who is an integral part of the Santa Barbara wine scene. Live lobsters are economically found at large-scale oriental groceries, and will stay alive if kept on ice or refrigerated for up to two days. (4 servings)

6 tablespoons unsalted butter
3 tablespoons extra virgin olive oil
1 leek, sliced thinly (white and light green portion only)
1 yellow onion, minced
1 stalk celery, minced
1 1/2 cups Aborio rice
5 cups chicken broth or water, warmed to a hot temperature
1/16 teaspoon saffron powder
1/2 teaspoon fresh thyme, chopped

Lobsters – 1 per person, 1 lb.each
Seasoned cooking water:
 2 bay leaves
 2 thyme stalks
 1 cup white wine
 Salt
 White pepper, crushed
 1 stalk celery, cut in 1/2" pieces
 1 yellow onion, cut in 1/2" pieces
 1 large carrot, cut in 1/2" pieces

1. Heat 4 tablespoons butter with the olive oil in a heavy sauce pan, and sauté the leek, onion and celery until softened.
2. Add the rice and stir until rice is thoroughly coated with butter and oil.
3. Add the stock, 1/2 cup at a time, stirring at each stage until the liquid has been completely absorbed before adding more, until all five cups have been used.
4. Continue stirring while cooking until done, between 30-40 minutes.
5. When done, add the saffron powder, thyme and remaining butter, and stir to combine.
6. Fill a pot large enough to hold all the lobsters 2/3 full of water, place all the herbs and vegetables into the water and bring to a boil.
7. Plunge the lobsters head first into the boiling water, cover, return to a boil and cook for 9 minutes or until done—lobsters will turn a bright red; do not overcook, or the meat will become tough.
8. Remove the lobsters from the water, let cool slightly, then using lobster or nut crackers, remove the meat from the tail and claws.
9. Serve the lobster meat on beds of the risotto.

THE WINE WITH THIS RECIPE

…has its glories pushed to higher levels. Its oak elements are elevated by the wonderful saffron influences, and the fruit gains bright discernability from the fullness in flavor from the lobster and risotto. Both wine and recipe make engagingly bold statements individually, and when combined give something worth shouting about!

Cakebread Cellars

NAPA VALLEY

Chardonnay

1994

CAKEBREAD CELLARS CHARDONNAY

...begins with a light golden color, and presents an attractive nose of pear, slight oak, and within minutes after breathing in the glass a soft, floral character that beautifully grows and grows. This solid Chardonnay provides hints of citrus as it opens in the mouth, its components meshing beautifully into a delicate wine that lasts with a finesse in its smooth finish. If Bruce Cakebread could bottle the feeling of a morning walk in the spring air of Napa as the vines begin to bud...this would come close.

SERVE WITH
SEA SCALLOPS WITH WARM SALAD OF SWEET CORN, ROAST PEPPER AND SHIITAKES WITH CHIVE OIL

Flavors of the land and of the sea combine with incredible grace in this recipe from the winery's resident chef, Brian Streeter, and Dolores

Cakebread. The barely-cooked sweet corn, the soft piquancy of the peppers, and the sublime earthiness of the mushrooms act as superb foils for the texture and taste of the scallops. Add this Cakebread glory from the grape, and this salad becomes merely spectacular. (8 servings)

CHIVE OIL
1 cup chives, chopped
2 cups vegetable oil
SALAD
2 shallots, minced
2 cloves garlic, minced
4 ears white corn, shucked and kerneled
3 red peppers, roasted and diced

1/2 pound shiitake mushrooms, sliced
1 tablespoon parsley, chopped
4 tablespoons butter
Salt, freshly ground pepper
2 pounds sea scallops, cleaned
4 ounces baby greens

1. Two hours before serving, purée chives and oil in blender on high speed until smooth. Reserve.
2. Sweat shallots and garlic in butter over medium heat until soft. Add corn, mushrooms, and peppers. Turn to high heat and season with salt, pepper, and parsley. Sauté to heat through and to soften mushrooms. Remove from heat and keep warm.
3. Brush scallops with oil and season with salt and pepper. Sear on both sides in a non-stick pan over high heat until brown.
4. Arrange a spoonful of corn salad in center of the plate. Top with three scallops. Arrange a small bundle of lettuce greens in the center to form a small bouquet. Drizzle with chive oil and serve.

THE WINE WITH THIS RECIPE
…becomes rarified, as it weaves into the flavors of the recipe and the recipe responds in kind. The touch of citrus comes alive, as does the floral essence and the lightly toasted barrel taste as it marries with the sweetness of the scallops. The bitterness of the greens works exceedingly well with the hints of vanilla from the oak, and overall the fruit in the wine becomes much bigger and fuller. Beyond all this, without a doubt, the more aged this wine gets, the more it will reveal and be revealed by this meal.

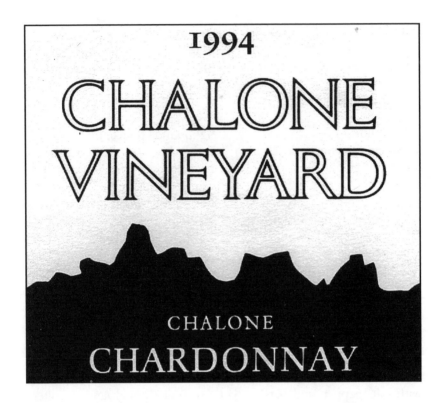

CHALONE VINEYARD CHARDONNAY

…is medium gold in the glass, with rich fruit aromas and hints of oak lending a soft vanilla tone. Its creaminess is evident in the nose, but in the mouth sustains a softness that embellishes its flavors.

SERVE WITH

SCALLOPS OF STRIPED BASS WITH TOMATO

Chef Angelo Auriano of Restaurante Valentino believes this to be a recipe "that can easily be made by an average cook…yet has a certain creativity that elevates it from the ordinary to the excellent." He also recommends any other kind of firm, white fish, such as Pacific Northwest halibut or swordfish (but never salmon). Most fish merchants will clean the fish for you, and filet them into the portions you need; simply ask for the head(s) in order to make your stock. (6 servings)

1 three pound striped bass (including the head)
2 cups water
1 clove garlic, chopped medium
1 scallion, chopped medium
1 stalk celery, chopped medium
1 carrot, chopped medium
4 tomatoes, peeled and chopped
1 bay leaf

$^1/_2$ cup flour (or as needed)
3 tablespoons olive oil
1 clove garlic, crushed
$^1/_3$ cup dry white wine
$^1/_4$ cup brandy
1 teaspoon Worcestershire sauce
$^1/_2$ cup sweet butter
6 basil leaves

1. Remove the scales and head from the fish and place them in a pot. Add the water, chopped garlic, scallions, celery, carrots, the first 2 chopped tomatoes, and the bay leaf. Bring the ingredients to a boil, and then simmer them for 1 hour. Occasionally skim off the top of the stock. Strain the stock through a cheesecloth and set it aside.

2. Cut the fish into 6 individual boneless steaks. Thoroughly coat them on both sides with the flour.

3. In a large skillet, place the olive oil and heat it on medium-high until it is hot. Add the crushed garlic. Add the floured fish steaks and sauté them for 1 minute on each side. Add the wine and brandy, and flambé them. Kill the heat, remove the fish steaks (reserve the liquid) and place them in a warm, covered dish.

4. Add the Worcestershire sauce, the other 2 chopped tomatoes, and the butter to the liquid in the skillet, and combine. Add the reserved stock, then stir the ingredients over a medium-high heat for 1-4 minutes, or until the liquid is reduced by half into a light sauce consistency.

5. Place one fish steak on each individual serving plate. Spoon the sauce over the top. Garnish the dish with a fresh basil leaf.

THE WINE WITH THIS RECIPE

...is a thing of beauty. The fruit is prevalent and expressive, and is enhanced by the meal. The wine sharpens its edge without becoming heavy, and by doing so is broadened, heightened and rounded by the process. In this way, the delicacy of the fish transforms the otherwise boldness of the wine, with the garlic influence adding its conductive two-cents worth as it finds and embraces the hints of oak. Finally, the smoothness of the wine and its finish becomes more thorough through this medium. In total, a fine example of complete culinary satisfaction.

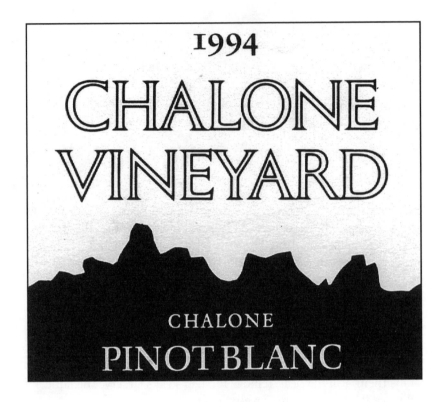

CHALONE VINEYARD PINOT BLANC

...is rich golden in color, and proffers a full-bodied aroma with hints of pear and fennel. Its feel is medium-rich and dry, round and creamy, with the pear and light fennel tones in force.

SERVE WITH
OYSTERS ROCKEFELLER-VAN LEUVEN

Although the original 1899 recipe for Oysters Rockefeller from Antoine's in New Orleans calls for whole oysters to be baked in the shell with the sauce on top, this adaptation uses lightly chopped oysters to more evenly spread out the flavors. Spinach can readily stand in for the preferred watercress; a teaspoon of freshly ground fennel seeds makes up for lack of the minced fresh, and one can use any anise-based liquor such as Sambuca instead of the pure Pernod. Hot pepper sauce is mandatory, either Tabasco or Tapatio. Cooking on the bed of salt helps diffuse the heat underneath the shells, plus the nesting keeps them stable as they cook. (4 servings, 3-4 per person)

6 T. unsalted butter, room temperature	lightly chopped
2 small shallots, minced	1/3-1/2 cup fresh bread crumbs
1 small leek (white part only), finely minced	2 tablespoons Pernod
	Salt to taste
1/4 cup finely minced fresh fennel	Hot pepper sauce, to taste
3 tablespoons minced fresh flat-leaf parsley	1-2 pounds rock salt
	8 ounces fresh oysters
1/2 teaspoon minced fresh tarragon	12-16 oyster shells
1 cup watercress, stems removed,	Lemon wedges

1. Heat 3 tablespoons butter in a skillet over medium heat. Add shallots and leek; cook, until shallots are just becoming translucent.
2. Add fennel, parsley, and tarragon; cook 3 minutes longer.
3. Stir in chopped watercress, toss while cooking until wilted, about 1 minute. Remove from heat, let cool slightly.
4. Stir in bread crumbs, Pernod, salt, and pepper sauce. Let mixture cool to room temperature, then stir in remaining 3 tablespoons butter.
5. Fold in chopped oysters, gently but thoroughly incorporating them throughout; add more bread crumbs if mixture becomes too liquidy.
6. Heat oven to 450°F.
7. Spread 1/2" layer of rock salt on baking sheets. Place a dollop of the oyster mix inside each shell. Sprinkle a dusting of bread crumbs on top, then arrange on the salt bed.
8. Bake for 4+ minutes, then place them under the broiler until the tops becomes golden brown.
9. Serve immediately, using tongs to remove the shells from their bed (scraping them a bit to knock off any salt that has barnacled to the shell).

THE WINE WITH THIS RECIPE

…becomes fresh-tasting, its buttery character emerging softly. The wine's balance of fruit and acid reacts well to the flavors of the oysters and shallots, plus the mild licorice flavor in the dish gently accents the mild fennel in the wine. This is a refined, well-appointed match.

CHATEAU MONTELENA
ESTABLISHED 1882

Chardonnay
NAPA VALLEY
1993

CHATEAU MONTELENA CHARDONNAY

...has a nice golden color, with delicate fruit in the nose, and suggests a nicely crafted, balanced Chardonnay, typical of its non-100% new oak style. This carries into the mouth, with rich impressions, with a gentle creaminess that embellishes its balance and sound structure. The dash of citrus keeps the finish clean and clear. Certainly a classy example of this winery's Chardonnay style.

BO'S ABALONE AUTÉNTICO

When abalone is in season, this is a simple way to prepare it, especially to enjoy cooking with and drinking the fine wines of Chateau Montelena. This recipe is the work of winemaker Bo Barrett, whose inspirations in the kitchen are as well regarded as his vinicultural accomplishments (and who prefers their Riesling in the marinade). Due to the fact that abalone is, to put it mildly, sometimes difficult to obtain, Bo suggests you try this same treatment for horse-neck clams, or as kabobs with shrimp or scallops. But there is a unique flavor that only abalone has, so if you aren't already, make friends with a diver! (3-4 servings)

1 medium abalone
2 tablespoons butter
3-4 tablespoons fresh basil
1 cup Chateau Montelena Chardonnay or Johannisberg Riesling
1-2 lemons, cut into wedges

1. Slice the abalone into $1/4$" thick steaks and gently pound.
2. Prepare the marinade by quickly melting the butter in a pan, adding the basil and the wine.
3. Place the seafood in a shallow dish and cover with the marinade, taking care to evenly distribute the basil over all. Marinate the seafood only long enough to prepare a very hot grill fire.
4. Grill the meat one minute on each side or until cooked to taste. Do not overcook abalone, unless you like nicely-flavored leather. Serve with lemon wedges.

THE WINE WITH THIS RECIPE
...has its richness and creaminess amplified, and its flavors rounded up and out! It makes for a complete mouth experience, as the fruit and flavors blend, swirl and complement each other, with the finish extending the life of the encounter. A very classic-tasting Chardonnay carried to another level, where its acids and its balance become the foundation for fresh excellence. This deserves high regard, Bo!

EDNA VALLEY VINEYARD

1991

Edna Valley

Chardonnay

Estate Bottled

Produced and bottled by
Edna Valley Vineyard
San Luis Obispo California USA
Alcohol 13.1% by volume

EDNA VALLEY VINEYARD CHARDONNAY
…has a deep golden color, with elements of wood/vanilla and crisp citrus in the nose, and an appealing, fruit aroma. It presents a roundness in the mouth, a medium-fullness, neither heavy nor light, with its citrusy character softly disclosed. A most inviting Chardonnay.

Serve with
CHICKEN, MUSHROOMS, CREAM AND TARRAGON

Calling for the more intense dark chicken meat, this dish has substance and spirit, with the zap of tarragon adding a touch out of the ordinary. A lovely recipe from the mind of Stephen Dooley, it's simple, rich and quick to make. (6 servings)

1/2 stick butter
6 chicken legs or thighs
8 ounces Italian brown mushrooms, sliced
1 cup chopped purple onion
1 teaspoon flour
1 cup chicken broth or stock
1 cup whipping cream
6-10 sprigs fresh tarragon
Salt, pepper

1. Melt butter in large frying pan.
2. Salt and pepper the chicken, pressing it into the skin.
3. Sauté the chicken pieces, 2-3 at a time, until definitely browned, approx. 4-6 minutes per side.
4. Remove, drain excess grease, then sauté the mushrooms and onion for 5 minutes.
5. Add the flour, cook 1-2 minutes, add broth, cream and tarragon, bring to a boil, and let boil for 10 minutes.
6. Reduce heat, return the chicken to the pan, and simmer for 30 minutes.
7. When chicken is thoroughly done, remove, reduce sauce as needed, and serve.

THE WINE WITH THIS RECIPE
…has its complexities enhanced and its fruity expression realized. The sauce works remarkably well, with the mushrooms bringing their classic earthiness to bear on the oak tones most complementarily. A graceful combination.

FISHER VINEYARDS CHARDONNAY
COACH INSIGNIA

...displays a beautiful golden color. Its nose delivers hints of fruit, of oak, balance—it smells like a good Chardonnay should. In the mouth, it expands nicely, slightly creamy with soft acids, a flash of citrus, and maintains a fine, lingering finish. After a few minutes in the glass, it expands magnificently, improving its already brilliant qualities.

SERVE WITH
GRILLED AHI WITH CILANTRO SAUCE
As conceived by Juelle Fisher, co-owner of the winery, the combina-

tion of soy sauce and sesame seed oil, along with the ginger, high-lights this marinated thick-flesh fish and makes for an Asian approach to a barbecue favorite. The complementary cilantro sauce with its echoes of the marinade furthers the flavors, and with this wine makes for an outdoor treat second to none. (6 servings)

MARINADE
$1/2$ cup rice wine vinegar
2 tablespoons soy sauce
1 tablespoon minced ginger
1 tablespoon sesame seed oil
CILANTRO SAUCE
3 tablespoons chicken broth or stock
3 tablespoons soy sauce
2 tablespoons sesame seed oil, light
$1^1/2$ tablespoons rice wine vinegar
1 tablespoon sugar
$1/2$ cup fresh cilantro, chopped

6 fresh ahi steaks

1. Combine the ingredients for the marinade, then marinate the ahi steaks for 8 hours in the refrigerator.
2. Whisk together the sauce ingredients, making sure the sugar is completely dissolved. Place near grill where fish will be cooked.
3. Grill steaks over red hot coals until desired doneness (slightly rare in middle is preferred at the winery), 4-5 minutes; it's best if the grill is oiled to prevent sticking. Pour sauce over the steaks when they come off the grill, and serve.

THE WINE WITH THIS RECIPE

...boosts the fine flavor of the fish, as its own creaminess is elevated. With the mild tinge of cilantro making a statement without overly doing so, the wine meshes with the full flavor of the fish, its marinade, and the sauce. The Chardonnay fruit is cleanly expressed, and almost seems to shine from the glass. A class act all the way.

GRGICH HILLS CHARDONNAY

...has a rich golden color, and presents even doses of pear and oak in the nose, extremely inviting aromas with just a touch of age. It opens well in the mouth, the acid ideally balancing the prevalent but not overbearing fruit and oak tones, and with its excellent finish this is a positively wonderful drinking wine.

SERVE WITH
CHICKEN WITH WILD MUSHROOMS AND WHITE WINE SAUCE

Ron Breitstein realized this would be absolutely appropriate for the flavors he detected in this wine. Not only that, he wanted to create something relatively easy to make. In keeping with that theme, he suggests this be served with lightly steamed asparagus (which can be briefly rolled, sauté style, in spiced oil just prior to serving) and sliced red potatoes. (4 servings)

4 boneless chicken breasts	3 tablespoons unsalted butter
Sea salt, freshly ground	1 pound assorted wild mushrooms
1 cup poultry stock	(portobello, shiitake, oyster),
1 cup Chardonnay (Grgich Hills)	lightly chopped
1/2 tablespoon chopped thyme	1/2 teaspoon cornstarch
1 tablespoon chopped tarragon	White pepper, freshly ground

1. Rinse and pat dry the chicken breasts, lightly pound to an even 3/8 –1/2" thickness, then lightly dust with fresh ground sea salt and refrigerate for two hours before cooking.
2. Put the stock in a small sauce pan, add the wine, thyme and tarragon, bring to a boil, and reduce by 2/3rds.
3. Melt 2 tablespoons of the butter in a medium skillet; when bubbly add the chicken breasts and cook until just opaque, about 90 seconds per side.
4. Remove to a 9" X 12" oven dish lined with foil, and fold the foil over to keep the meat warm.
5. Preheat the oven to 350°F.
6. Add the remaining tablespoon of butter to the pan, add the mushrooms, and sauté for 3-4 minutes, until the mushrooms begin to just glaze. Open the foil just long enough to spread the mushrooms over the chicken, and recover with the foil.
7. Place a small portion of the sauce into a small sealable container, add the cornstarch, shake to mix thoroughly, then add to rest of sauce. Bring sauce to a light simmer and stir until it coats the spoon.
8. Reopen the chicken package, pour the sauce over all, reseal, then place dish in the oven and bake for 10 minutes.
9. Place each breast portion on a plate, slather with the mushrooms and sauce, and serve.

THE WINE WITH THIS RECIPE

...deliciously broadens in scope. The tarragon influence enlivens the fruit, and the earthiness of the mushrooms heightens the oak and earthiness waiting in the wine. The sauce additionally accents the roundness and complexity in the wine, making it richer and fuller. Both wine and recipe clearly enjoy the other's company!

JORDAN CHARDONNAY

...has a fine golden hue, and releases a full, attractive nose, with oak elements that are not too overblown. Flashes of pear, melon, a touch of orange blossom appears, hinting at a delightfully fruity wine. In the mouth, it reveals an even, medium-creamy body, with excellent fruit tones that blossom on the tongue. Citrus is released in the finish, accenting the soft acids in this extremely well-balanced, ready-to-drink-now wine.

SERVE WITH

CORN PANCAKES WITH SMOKED SALMON BUTTER

This combination of the sweetness of corn and the savor of smoked salmon is deceptively tasty and surprisingly light. The butter can be prepared well in advance, and can also be the inspiration for other uses, such as a condiment on cucumbers, or a replacement for other sauces such as Hollandaise. This recipe came from the winery and as might be expected they know how to mate their wines with food. (8 servings)

CORN PANCAKES
2 medium potatoes
1 cup milk
3 ears of fresh white or yellow corn
Ice water
3 tablespoons flour
2 eggs
1 egg white
Salt and pepper
Dollop of butter

SMOKED SALMON BUTTER
$1/2$ pound unsalted butter, soft
$1/2$ pound smoked salmon
3 tablespoons heavy whipping cream
Salt and pepper
Lemon juice

Crème fraîche (or crema Mexicana)
$1/2$ cup chives, chopped
Caviar

TO PREPARE CORN PANCAKES
1. Peel, quarter and boil potatoes in salted water. Drain, purée in processor, then pass through a sieve to eliminate lumps.
2. Cut kernels from 2 ears of corn and simmer in milk for about 5 minutes. When cool, purée the corn and milk in a food processor or

blender; pass the purée through a fine sieve and reserve the corn-flavored milk, discarding the corn residue.

3. Remove the kernels from the third ear of corn and cook them in boiling, salted water for 3-4 minutes. Drain the corn kernels and cool in ice water. When cool, remove from water and set aside.

4. Whisk corn-flavored milk into the potato purée, then gradually add flour, the two eggs (one at a time), and the egg white. Season with salt and pepper.

5. Brush a well-seasoned pan with butter, and heat to medium-hot. When hot, lightly apply a coating of non-stick vegetable spray, then pour in about 3 tablespoons of batter to form a 4" diameter pancake (depending on thickness of batter, you may need to tilt the pan to distribute the batter evenly). When the first side of the pancake has set, about 2 minutes, distribute 7-13 cooked kernels of corn over the top of the pancake and lightly press into surface. Cook an additional 2-3 minutes, or until browned; flip over, being careful to maintain pancake shape as they can be extremely delicate, and finish cooking second side. Keep pancakes warm as you cook additional servings, using non-stick spray for each session; a tortilla warmer works well at keeping them ready before serving.

To make salmon butter

1. Purée smoked salmon in food processor or blender for about 30 seconds.

2. Add butter and process until fully incorporated.

3. Blend in cream and season with salt, pepper, and lemon juice, to taste.

4. Pass through a sieve to remove lumps. (This will keep in the refrigerator for up to 2 weeks; bring to room temperature before using.)

To assemble

1. Place about 1 tablespoon of smoked salmon butter between two warm corn pancakes.

2. Garnish top with a small amount of crème fraîche and chopped chives, then touch off with a small serving of caviar, providing a supply at table for those who desire more.

THE WINE WITH THIS RECIPE

...has its creaminess increased. The pleasant salmon flavor and the natural citrus of the wine blend well. Also, the sweetness of the white corn interacts with the fruit in a very stimulating way. With the chives bringing out fresh oak characteristics as well, which in turn deliciously bounces off the salmon, the wine and food flavors linger into a smooth and lasting finish.

KISTLER CHARDONNAY
DUTTON RANCH

...features a deep, rich, golden color. The nose is big and beautiful, lots of fruit and oak, as balanced as the finest French Burgundy gets, perhaps even more elegant. The mouth feel is luxuriant, as hints of apricot, peach, and pear appear, simply gorgeous fruit with a great acid counterbalance. The wine seems to glide down the throat, leaving a memorable finish.

SERVE WITH

SEARED WHITEFISH WITH FRENCH FRIES "NOT FRIED," ROASTED GARLIC CLOVES AND BRANDADE

Famed chef Joachim Splichal of the Patina/Pinot Restaurant group tendered this tantilizing tour-de-force. It is presented here in its various stages; some can be done somewhat simultaneously, but there are patient timing elements that are unavoidable if all is to be done right. The "French fry" section actually produces two contributions, small blocks of potato that are used in the "jus," and batonnets that mimic the look of traditional French fries, both of which are boiled to just shy of being completely done, and are served together as a sort of frame for the fish and brandade. (4 servings)

POTATO JUS
1/4 cup unsalted butter
1 Idaho potato, peeled and cut into 1/2" cubes
1 onion, cut into 1/2" cubes
1 medium leek, white part only, cut into 1/2" cubes
2 ribs celery, cut into 1/2" cubes
4 cloves garlic, unpeeled
1 sprig fresh thyme
1/4 teaspoon whole white peppercorns
2 cups chicken stock

"FRENCH FRIES"
1 Idaho potato, peeled and cut into 1/4" cubes
1 Idaho potato, peeled and cut into 1/3"-1/3"-31/2" "batonnets"
  (makes 16)

BRANDADE
4 ounces whitefish filet, skin on
2 cups milk
1 large Idaho potato, peeled and quartered
1/4 cup unsalted butter
1/4 cup heavy cream (or milk)
Salt, freshly ground white pepper
4 tablespoons quadruple-blanched garlic puree*

WHITEFISH
1/4 cup extra virgin olive oil
2 tablespoons all-purpose flour
Salt, freshly ground white pepper
Four 4 ounce portions whitefish filet, skin on

1/3 cup extra-virgin olive oil
2 tablespoons finely chopped chives
Salt, freshly ground white pepper

To make Potato Jus (approx. 95 minutes)

1. In a large, heavy saucepan, melt the butter over medium-low heat. Add the potato, onion, leek, celery, garlic, thyme and whole peppercorns. Sweat the vegetables slowly, stirring occasionally, for about 20 minutes or until very soft but not browned.

2. Add the stock, bring to a simmer, partially cover, and cook slowly for 45 minutes. (If the stock reduces too much, add up to 1 cup of water to keep the level about the same.)

3. Pass the stock through a fine strainer into a small saucepan, pressing down hard on the solids to extract all their flavor; discard the solids. Over high heat, boil the liquid until reduced to about $1/2$ cup, skimming off the fat with a large flat spoon. Set the pan aside, covered, until you are ready to finish the dish.

To make "French Fries" (approx. 20 minutes)

1. Placing the 2 different sizes of potato in their own separate saucepans, combine them with a generous amount of cold water, and bring them both to a boil over medium-high heat. Cook until the potatoes are tender but not falling apart—4 minutes for the cubes and 6 minutes for the batonnets. Remove the pans from the heat and allow to cool.

2. Drain the potato cubes well and add them to the reserved potato jus.

3. Drain the batonnets and set them aside on a lightly buttered baking sheet until you are ready for the final assembly.

To make the Brandade (approx. 50 minutes)

1. Preheat the oven to 400°F.

2. Place the whitefish in a lightly oiled roasting pan and roast for about 6 minutes, or until firm and cooked through. Remove the skin and mash the fish with a fork until well broken up. Set aside.

3. Place the milk and quartered potatoes in a large saucepan, making up the level with water if necessary so that all the potatoes are covered, and bring to a boil. Cook for 20-25 minutes, or until tender.

4. When the potatoes are done, drain and pass them through a food mill or mash with a masher or a hand blender—do not use a food processor.

5. Place mashed potatoes in a clean pan. In a separate small saucepan, bring the butter and cream to a boil. Slowly add this mixture to the potatoes, stirring all the time, over low heat.

6. Stir in the mashed whitefish and the garlic puree*. Season to taste with salt and pepper, cover, and set aside until you are ready to assemble the dish.

*QUADRUPLE-BLANCHED GARLIC PUREE: *Take approx. 8-10 peeled cloves of garlic, place in small saucepan, cover with cold water. Bring water to a boil, then drain. Recover garlic cloves with cold water, bring to fresh boil, drain again. Repeat two more times (4 times in all), then purée.*

TO PREPARE THE WHITEFISH (APPROX. 9 MINUTES)
1. Preheat the oven to 400°F.
2. On a plate, blend together the flour with salt and pepper, to taste. Lightly coat the skin side of the fish filets with the flour mixture and shake off any excess.
3. In a large, oven-proof sauté pan, heat the oil over medium-high heat. When the oil is very hot, fry the fish, skin side down, for about 4 minutes or until the skin is dark brown and crispy. Turn the fish to the other side and place the pan in the oven to finish cooking for 2-3 minutes, or until the fish is firm.
4. Remove the fish, but leave the oven on; set the fish aside at the back of the stove, uncovered, while you finish the sauce and garnish.

TO ASSEMBLE THE DISH (APPROX. 7 MINUTES)
1. Reheat the baking sheet of potato batonnets in the still-running oven for about 3 minutes, or until hot.
2. Bring the potato jus to a simmer, add the oil and bring to a fast boil, stirring, so that the oil emulsifies with the jus.
3. Remove from the heat, add chives and season with salt and white pepper.
4. Gently reheat the brandade, if necessary.
5. On each of 4 large heated plates, mound some of the brandade in the center and top with a filet of whitefish, skin side up.
6. Place 4 batonnets in a square around each serving and spoon a little of the sauce, with its potato cubes, over each of the "fries."

THE WINE WITH THE RECIPE
...*becomes even more incredibly spectacular. The roundness and richness creates a spell in the mouth, as all the flavors, all the complexities, become a series of taste tableaux, one after another, all different, all superb.*

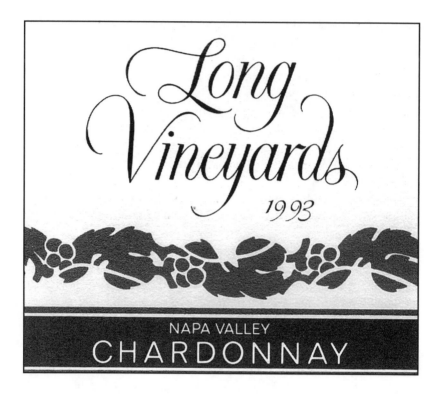

LONG VINEYARDS CHARDONNAY

…is rich golden in color, with a wonderfully opulent nose revealing striking balance between the oak, the fruit and the acid. The vanilla extract from the French oak lends a creaminess, like a soft lemon custard. It fills out the mouth nicely, with expansive fruit from start to finish, which delightfully stays with you. The subtle oak is attractive, the fruit prominent yet not overbearing, plus there's a delicious edge from the acid. A truly pleasurable wine to drink.

SERVE WITH

CRAYFISH AND YELLOW TOMATO BISQUE

A creation from the brilliant chef Robert Grenner, its only stumbling block is obtaining fresh crayfish (aka crawfish). Although you should pre-cook the crayfish a la lobster, it is obtainable in a cooked-fresh form from some full-service gourmet grocers. Once these fresh-water spiny lobsters are cooked and the tail meat extracted, it only takes about $1^1/_2$ hours to make this soup from there, and it's a wow! (4-6 servings)

$1/_4$ cup canola oil
2 pounds crayfish, cooked, tail meat removed
3-4 pounds yellow tomatoes, chopped
2 purple onions, chopped
$1/_2$ bunch basil, chopped
$1/_3$ head of celery, chopped
$1/_3$ cup shallots, chopped
$1/_8$ cup garlic, chopped
1-2 teaspoons cayenne pepper
$1/_2$ bottle dry white wine (Long Chardonnay)
2 ounces brandy
Pinch of saffron
2 tablespoons water
2 cups cream
Salt, pepper
Sour cream (optional)

1. Sauté half the crayfish meat, tomatoes, onion, basil, celery, shallot, garlic and pepper in canola oil for 5 minutes.
2. Add wine and brandy to soup base, and simmer over a light flame for 45 minutes, stirring occasionally. Remove from heat to cool slightly.
3. In a small bowl, put pinch of saffron in water to soak.
4. Purée the soup base, then strain through a fine sieve, discarding solids.
5. Return soup to heat in a large pan, add saffron, cream, and remaining crayfish meat. Simmer 15 minutes, stirring frequently.
6. Add salt and pepper to taste, and serve in individual bowls, making sure to include a good portion of the crayfish meat. Add a dollop of sour cream in the center of each serving, if desired.

THE WINE WITH THIS RECIPE

...becomes even more round and full. The cayenne picks up on the oak in the wine, the saffron and cream accentuate its fullness, and the crayfish flavor is positively benefitted by the association with the Chardonnay fruit. The texture of the wine blends naturally with that of the soup, and proves to be a splendid match.

LOUIS M. MARTINI CHARDONNAY
Reserve

...features a beautiful light golden color. There's a rich full nose, hints of toasty oak, slightly crisp with evident fruit, distinctively Chardonnay. Reveals nice body weight in mouth, the oak becomes very complementary, and the fruit of the grape a definite. The finish luxuriates, bringing an auxiliary texture that completes and satisfies.

Serve with
Golden Coquille St. Jacques

For scallop lovers, this is a classy version of Coquille St. Jacques made a touch more elegant by the inclusion of golden caviar. Essentially scallops cooked in a quick and simple vegetable/wine stock, this main course was created by Elizabeth Martini, and shows how great family life can be! (6 servings)

2 cups dry white wine (Louis Martini)
1 cup water
1 cup mixed, sliced vegetables:
  yellow onion, carrot and celery
1 bay leaf
4 whole allspice
6 whole peppercorns
1^1/2 pounds fresh scallops, medium-large
Salt, freshly ground white pepper
1 cup sour cream
^{1}/2 tablespoon fresh lemon juice
4 ounces golden caviar
1/4 cup green onion, chopped
6-8 lemon wedges

1. In a small, heavy saucepan, add the wine, water, mixed vegetables, bay leaf, allspice and peppercorns. Bring to a boil, lower heat, and simmer about 20 minutes. While the vegetables cook, rinse and dry the scallops and lightly season with salt and pepper.
2. Strain the vegetable stock, bring it back to the boil, plunge in the scallops and turn them once or twice until mixture comes to another boil and scallops just turn opaque. Remove the scallops immediately—do not overcook. (If desired, cut the scallops into smaller pieces.) Set aside to cool.
3. Mix sour cream until smooth, and cream in a little lemon juice. Toss scallops in this sauce until well-coated.
4. Top each serving of sauce-laden scallops with a teaspoon of caviar and garnish with chopped green onion and a wedge of lemon. Place a small dish with remaining caviar on the table for those wishing more.

THE WINE WITH THIS RECIPE

...provides delightful accompaniment. The oak is still prevalent, but not overpowering, and this intensifies the creamy qualities of the wine. Along with the great mouth feel, the fruit stands out more significantly, and its substantial points mesh with the dish. Three taste treats of the world, scallops, caviar and Chardonnay, are well stated in this combination.

1994
NAPA VALLEY
CHARDONNAY
RESERVE
UNFILTERED
ROBERT MONDAVI WINERY
PRODUCED AND BOTTLED BY ROBERT MONDAVI WINERY
OAKVILLE, CALIFORNIA, PRODUCE OF USA

ROBERT MONDAVI WINERY CHARDONNAY
RESERVE

…is medium golden in color, with a full-bodied nose, revealing hints of pineapple and pear along with great grape essences—lots of fruit! Has an immediate plush mouth feel, displays typically fine balance, with a rich, persistent finish. With its subtle elegance, one of the most complete wines of its class.

SERVE WITH
CHIVE CANNELLONIS WITH PRAWN AND SHIITAKE FILLING

A hand-crafted dish from top to bottom. It requires a food processor and pasta machine, but is a lot easier than it sounds. The beauty of this recipe is that this can be an elegant first course or the center of a meal. The creation of Mondavi Executive Chef Sarah Scott, it's elaborate, but well worth the effort. (8 servings)

PASTA
1¹/₂ cups flour
1 egg
1 egg white
1 tablespoon olive oil
1 teaspoon kosher salt
Water
1 bunch chives, chopped fine
Parchment paper

FILLING
1 pound prawns, cleaned and deveined, chopped coarsely
2 tablespoons butter
1 tablespoon olive oil
3 shallots, chopped fine
2 cloves of garlic, chopped fine
1 pound shiitake mushrooms, sliced
¹/₄ cup basil leaves, cut into chiffonade
¹/₈ cup cognac
¹/₃ cup Chardonnay
¹/₂ cup heavy cream

SAUCE
2 cups heavy cream
1 cup Chardonnay
1 cup fish stock
2 shallots chopped fine

1 stalk of basil, cut into chiffonade, for garnish

TO MAKE THE PASTA
1. In food processor, combine flour, egg, egg white, olive oil and salt. Process with metal blade until thoroughly combined (dough will be like tiny beads).
2. Add chives, process 5 seconds.
3. Then, with machine running, slowly dribble in water, stopping just as dough comes to a ball.
4. Remove dough, shape into a ball (if it is a bit wet, just knead in

some flour), wrap in plastic wrap and let rest in refrigerator about 30 minutes.

To prepare the cannellonis

1. Cut dough in quarters, pass each piece through a pasta machine, folding and kneading the dough the first few times, then begin decreasing the thickness until you have a thin sheet of dough.
2. Lay out the dough strips on a floured surface and let dry about 5-10 minutes.
3. Using a cardboard or thick paper rectangle cut 3"x 4" as a template, cut the pasta into as many pieces as possible; excess pasta can be reprocessed for more sheets.
4. Heat a large pot of water to boiling, add a touch of salt and olive oil, and return to the boil.
5. Drop in sheets of pasta, and cook about 1 minute, then drain and immediately plunge pasta sheets into cold water.
6. Lift them out, shake off excess water, and place on a sheet pan lined with parchment paper until ready to be filled, 6-8 a layer, stacking with parchment paper shelving to keep them separate. (These can be kept covered in the refrigerator overnight.)

To make filling

1. In a large sauté pan, heat butter and olive oil over medium high heat, careful not to burn. Toss in prawns and sauté quickly until just pink.
2. Remove prawns from pan immediately and set aside.
3. Add shallots and garlic to pan, and sauté over medium heat until soft and golden.
4. Add mushrooms, increase the heat, and sauté for about 3 minutes until limp.
5. Splash in the cognac and wine, and reduce by almost half.
6. Stir in the basil and cream, and continue to reduce until mixture is thickened.
7. Remove from heat, let cool, then stir in prawns. Add salt and pepper to taste.

To make sauce

1. In one saucepan, over medium heat reduce cream down to one cup.

2. In a separate pan combine wine and fish stock, and reduce to one cup of liquid.

3. Combine cream, wine/fish stock/shallots and basil, and continue to simmer over medium to low heat until thickened.

4. Strain and season with salt and pepper to taste. (Can be enriched with butter at the end.)

To assemble

1. Spoon about 1-1^1/2 tablespoons filling in center of pasta sheet. Carefully roll around filling to create stuffed tube, and place in shallow baking dish (9" x 13").

2. Continue with rest of filling and pasta sheets; you should wind up with between 16-24 cannellonis.

3. Drizzle a bit of the sauce over the cannellonis and bake in a 425°F oven for 10-15 minutes or until heated through; for the final minute, you can run them under the broiler if desired.

4. To serve, place 2 cannellonis on a plate, nap with hot sauce, and sprinkle with chiffonade of basil.

The wine with this recipe

...actually becomes even smoother and more velvety! The brandy meshes well with the food, and enhances the fruit qualities and the wine's inherent creaminess. The combination of earth, sea and wine generates a complete experience, and furthers the wine's finish. An outstanding wine meets an outstanding recipe, and the results are gloriously remarkable.

SANFORD CHARDONNAY
BARREL SELECT

...has a medium golden color, and features a creamy nose, bold fruit, and a radiant aroma. An enormously rich feel in the mouth, excellent Chardonnay character, hints of citrus within its lush and plush feel, almost a breath of enticing herbaceousness. A long, lingering finish. Simply a most spectacular wine.

SERVE WITH
PLUSH PISTACHIO CHICKEN BREASTS

One of the most successful matches in the book, the combination of the nuts, cream and chicken is incredibly complemented by the flavors in this wine. This recipe was crafted by Shirley Sarvis especially for this winery, and we think it's an instant classic. (4 servings)

2 medium-large frying chicken breasts, split, boned, and skinned
 (approx. 1 pound meat)
Salt and freshly ground white pepper
3+ tablespoons unsalted butter
1/2 cup Sanford Chardonnay

1 cup heavy whipping cream
$^1/_2$ - $^3/_4$ cup chopped and toasted fresh pistachios

1. Lightly pound breast pieces to an even 5/8" thickness. Season with salt and pepper.
2. Heat butter in a large, heavy frying pan over medium heat until it bubbles well. Add breasts and cook, occasionally turning until meat becomes opaque almost to the center, about 6 minutes total. Remove to serving plates, keep warm.
3. Remove excess butter from pan. Add wine, cook over high heat, lightly stirring, until reduced by half; add cream, cook and stir until liquid reduces to a very heavy cream consistency. Season with salt and pepper. Spoon over breasts, then sprinkle each serving with nuts.

THE WINE WITH THIS RECIPE
…is beautifully matched, everything complementary. The smoothness of the citrus flavor meshes easily with the cream sauce, and the flavors from the toasted pistachio glide into the vanilla and oak, so that all combines majestically. In plain English, this works great!

SIMI WINERY CHARDONNAY

...is light-medium gold in color, with evident fruit and citrus along with pleasant oak in nose. The mouth feel has medium body weight, is well-balanced, and succinctly delivers its clues of citrus and oak. The finish maintains the theme of restrained excellence, by not carrying things too far. As expected, it exemplifies the solid, well-grounded approach to Chardonnay that is the hallmark of Simi.

SERVE WITH

SHRIMP, CORN AND RED BEAN SALAD

This multi-faceted salad is a cooling alternative to picnic slaws and potato salads, with the zest of green onions, the sweetness of corn, the smoothness of beans, and the pleasure of shrimp. The remoulade sauce is also keepable, and can be used on other salads or for seafood cocktails. This recipe comes from Mary Evely, Simi Chef par excellence, who suggests that crawfish when in season makes a wonderful substitute for the shrimp. (6 servings)

24 cooked and shelled shrimp
4 ears of corn
1 cup cooked small red beans
4 green onions, white and green parts, sliced into rounds
3 tablespoons vinaigrette (your favorite recipe)
12 leaves of butter lettuce or other appropriate salad green
1 cup remoulade sauce:
    4 medium cornichon pickles, chopped fine
    1 tablespoon capers, rinsed and drained
    2 teaspoons Dijon mustard
    2 tablespoons chopped fresh herbs—chives, tarragon and
        Italian parsley
    $1/2$ cup mayonnaise (or less)
    $1/2$ cup sour cream (or less)

1. Cut the raw corn from the ears and place in a bowl with the beans and green onions.
2. Toss with the vinaigrette.
3. Mix together the remoulade ingredients and spread a spoonful of this dressing in the middle of 6 plates.
4. Place two leaves of lettuce on top of each, and mound some of the corn mixture on top.
5. Place another spoonful of the remoulade at the side of the plate, arrange four shrimp around it, and serve.

THE WINE WITH THIS RECIPE

…becomes elevated and has its themes of citrus and oak turned into a full composition. The sweet tones of the corn, beans and shrimp bring out the body in the oak with style, and the tang of the remoulade make the lemon beauty more refined. The bite from the green onions creates a fresh edge to the wine, and as the finish clears the palate it brings the experience full circle and sets up the foundation for another bite and sip. And another bite and sip. And another…!

WILD HORSE

1994
CHARDONNAY
CENTRAL COAST

WILD HORSE CHARDONNAY

…has a light-medium straw color, with hints of pear and oak in the nose, its crisp fruit emanating into the senses. Smooth to the taste, it expresses a subdued vanilla that is wrapped in a touch of citrus, presenting an almost lemon custard quality. It displays good body weight, a gentle elegance, and is extremely well-balanced as it calmly finishes off.

SERVE WITH
FETTUCCINE WITH SAFFRON CREAM

A spring celebration! The peas thaw in the heat of the asparagus, lending an extra snap to the vegetables, and with the intensity of the saffron and the color and flavor of the roasted peppers, this dish is complete and sophisticated. This is the creation of Tricia Volk, co-owner of the winery and an accomplished cookbook author. (6 servings)

1/2 teaspoon saffron threads
3 tablespoons dry white wine
1 pound asparagus, washed, trimmed, and cut into 2" pieces
Salt, to taste
1 package (10 ounces) frozen peas
1 tablespoon unsalted butter
2 shallots, peeled and finely minced
1 1/2 cups heavy whipping cream
Salt and freshly ground black pepper, to taste
2 roasted red bell peppers, peeled and cut into long strips
1 teaspoon finely grated lemon zest
1 pound dried fettuccine, preferably imported Italian
1 cup freshly grated Parmesan cheese.

1. In a small bowl, put the saffron threads in the wine, let soak for 15 minutes.
2. Bring a large stock pot of water to boil over high heat. When the water reaches a rolling boil, add salt and the asparagus and cook until the asparagus are just crisp-tender. Add the peas to the asparagus and then drain the contents into a colander. Set aside.
3. In a large saucepan over medium heat, add the butter and the shallots and cook for about 5 minutes. Add the saffron threads and wine, and cook until the wine is reduced by 50%. Add the cream, salt, black pepper, red bell peppers and lemon zest, and continue to cook until the sauce is slightly reduced, about 5 minutes. Add the asparagus and peas and keep warm while the pasta cooks. Taste and correct seasonings.
4. Bring a large stock pot of water to boil over high heat. When the water reaches a rolling boil add the pasta and cook it just past the al dente stage. Drain the pasta and transfer to a large warmed serving platter. Pour the Saffron Cream over the fettuccine and sprinkle the Parmesan over the top. Toss well so that the pasta is coated with the sauce. Serve immediately.

THE WINE WITH THIS RECIPE
…has its creaminess brought forward with astounding results. The smooth, fruit flavors determine a lushness with the food, with the glances from the lemon zest memorably reflected in the wine. The flavors of the garden meld with the flavors in the wine, and prove to be an excellent match.

R I E S L I N G

THE DAYS OF RIESLINGS as purely sweet wines are passing. True, there are a number of California producers who still adhere to the original methods as championed along the shores of the Rhine in Germany, creating acid sweet wines of rich luxuriousness that rival the nectars that come from Deutschland. However, countless other winemakers are developing "dryer," more austere styles of Riesling that may create an entirely new trend in the United States. Whatever your tastes, there are wines and recipes that can match any style of wine you prefer—or care to experience.

Riesling has a long, long association with the Rhine and Mosel areas of Germany. In the 15th Century, shortly after the 30 Years War (1618-1648), the Catholic Church put political pressure on the bulk-type wine growers of the area to concentrate only on the Riesling. It may have been heavy-handed, but it worked. As Hugh Johnson pointedly states in his book *Vintage*, Riesling "...is hardy against all weathers; it ripens late...[plus] it achieves exceptional sweetness while maintaining a high degree of (extremely tasty) acidity. When [sweetness and acidity] are concentrated in a small crop the wine maintains its balance of intense yet transparent flavours for improbably long periods of time." Not only that, it occasionally benefits from a mold, "botrytis cinerea," that can accidentally hit at harvest time, which intensifies and maximizes the sugar content without affecting the acids, and so the Ausleses, Beerenausleses, and the ultimate Trockenbeerenausleses, (sweet, more deeply sweet, and extremely nectarish, respectively), are made possible.

Because the true "White Riesling" occasionally gets confused with the Sylvaner and other Germanic wines that are sometimes casually referred to as Riesling, it has therefore become almost universally known as Johannisberg Riesling to help keep it separate from the pack.

Dry, sweet, somewhere in between, Johannisberg Riesling is a wonderfully accessible wine, one that brings pleasure by itself or, certainly, with food. It's been long held that Riesling goes well with such food as sweet-meated Dungeness crab, steamed cockles, mussels, sand dabs, and other fish and shellfish. Who knows what else may come to mind? Prosit!

BOTRYTIS *Long Vineyards* 1993

NAPA VALLEY
JOHANNISBERG RIESLING
NATURAL SUGAR AT HARVEST 25° BRIX
RESIDUAL SUGAR AFTER FERMENTATION 12.5% BY WEIGHT
GROWN, PRODUCED, AND BOTTLED BY LONG VINEYARDS
BOX 50, ST. HELENA, CA • ALCOHOL 7% BY VOLUME

LONG VINEYARDS JOHANNISBERG RIESLING

…has a light, golden color. Its beautiful, floral nose promises sweetness and apricots with a flash of vanilla. It's like drinking fresh, scintillating grape juice, the apricot and pear features emerging, a wine well-balanced between fruit and acid. An incredible taste treat.

PAPAYA WITH CAVIAR

This wild combination comes from the imaginative mind of Bob Long, who envisioned replacing the black seeds in the center of papaya with classic beluga caviar. This "recipe" works just as well with a large papaya cut into serving portions as it does with the suggested normal size. Without a doubt, these three flavors are best when served together, because united, they stand! (4 servings)

Papaya, 1/2 per person
4 ounces caviar
Lime wedges
Long Vineyards Johannisberg Riesling

Wash, pat dry, then cut each papaya in half. Scoop out the black seeds until all traces are gone, along with any strings or membranes. Place a small dollop of caviar into this cavity, drizzle with some of the wine, and serve with the lime wedges, along with the remaining caviar for those who desire larger portions.

THE WINE WITH THIS RECIPE
...actually has its remarkable sweetness excitingly intensified! Like an assembly of assertive, independent flavors, each component clearly presents itself yet complements the others, and combined they swirl inside the mouth like a gentle tropical hurricane.

TREFETHEN NAPA RIESLING

...is light straw in color, and its aromas provide dry hints of fruit, citrus, a mild pungency, fresh table grape, slight honeydew, a fresh spring morning. Excellent, well-balanced feel in the mouth, smooth and dry. This is a classy, mellow wine with an outstanding finish.

SERVE WITH
SAFFRON DUNGENESS CRAB BISQUE

Janet Trefethen furnished this recipe, which has substance from the sea and a touch of Indian exotica. Although not separately featured here, she also recommended another simple meal involving crab and this wine. In fact, it's one of her family's favorite finger foods: a whole cooked crab, artichokes, a baguette of sweet bread, and the wine. However, this soup is clever and complex, a beautiful statement of flavors tailored to accompany this superb white wine. (8 servings)

2 Dungeness crabs, blanched
1/4 cup corn oil
2 cups diced leeks
2 cups diced onions
1 cup diced carrots
2 cups diced celery
1 tablespoon saffron threads
1 tablespoon tomato paste
2 quarts fish stock
1 bay leaf
8 peppercorns
1 head garlic

1 bunch each parsley, tarragon, thyme—separate leaves and stems
2 cups rice
1 quart heavy cream

GARNISH

4 cups leeks, julienned and crisp fried
4 ounces heavy cream, whipped
1/8 cup each parsley, thyme and chives, minced

1. Remove all meat from crab and reserve.
2. Cover crab shells in towel and, with a mallet, break into small pieces.
3. Heat large stock pot with corn oil. Add diced leeks, onion and carrots, and cook until lightly browned.
4. Stir in celery, saffron, crab shells, tomato paste; cook a few minutes more.
5. Pour in fish stock; add bay leaf, peppercorns, garlic and stems from parsley, tarragon and thyme. Bring mixture to simmer and cook 1 1/2 hours.
6. Strain, discarding solids.
7. Rinse rice and add to saffron crab stock. Cook until just tender, about 10-15 minutes.
8. Add in cream and reduce until liquid measures about 4 cups.
9. Purée with electric beaters or round wand.
10. Add reserved crab meat.
11. Chop leaves reserved from parsley, tarragon and thyme, and season soup to taste with herbs, salt and pepper.
12. Ladle soup into serving bowls. Garnish with dollop of whipped cream, fried leeks and a pinch of minced herbs.

THE WINE WITH THIS RECIPE

…forms a stylish complement to the soup, as its acids are drawn slightly forward while maintaining its complete smoothness. The fruit flavor is active, as the lushness of the soup wheels around the mouth; the wine helps ease some of the thickness inherent in bisques, creating a residue of flavors in the finish that draws one to have spoonful after spoonful. A glorious pairing.

GEWÜRZTRAMINER

*G*EWÜRZ MEANS "SPICY" in German, and such is the generic nature of this most floral and fragrant wine. The California style of late has been to make it dryer than its Alsatian counterparts, while still retaining much of its charm and appeal. It is quietly earning a place for itself among wine lovers, who enjoy its unique flavor characteristics: allspice, rose water, nutmeg, cinnamon, sage, citrus peel. It is virtually the only wine to serve with traditional bread-stuffed Thanksgiving turkey (especially barbecued using the domed indirect-heat method), as it catches and matches most of the flavors therein.

It is interesting to note that its genetic base, the Traminer, is not a wildly successful wine grape, making pleasant vin ordinaire in its European homes of Alsace, Germany and the Tyrol, but with the added spark that spice can bring, it becomes much improved indeed as the Gewürztraminer. Not only are the natural wines made from it engaging, alluring, and enormously appealing, they can be gloriously transformed by a lovely mold that can form on the grapes if it rains during harvest time, botrytis cinerea, "the noble rot," that dehydrates the grapes on the vine, concentrates the sugars, and produces late-harvest intensities in the same fashion as Sauternes and Trockenbeerenausleses.

A great Gewürztraminer is one of the joys in life.

BABCOCK VINEYARDS GEWÜRZTRAMINER

…enjoys a light-golden color. The Alsatian-style nose is enticing, and features hints of lichee nut and sweet spices, the fruit almost jumping out the glass. There is soft spice in the mouth, quite delicate, and the fruit is subtle yet prevalent. The finish maintains the tones of spice, and helps round out what is clearly a user-friendly, drinkable wine.

SERVE WITH
GINGERED PRAWNS WITH SCALLION RISOTTO

Mona Babcock, co-owner of the winery, created this spectacular taste-combination to accompany this wine. Among Italians, cooking risotto is considered an art; in this case, the addition of the green onions adds an appropriate accent to the ginger-laden shrimp. When presented with the recommended scallion "flowers," this dish makes an eye-catching entree. (4-6 servings) (Pictured on cover)

4 cups cooked scallion risotto:
  1/8 cup olive oil
  1/4 cup red onion, minced
  3/4 cup scallions, sliced
  1 tablespoon garlic, minced
  1 cup aborio rice

2 cups chicken stock - hot
1/4 teaspoon white pepper
4 tablespoons rice vinegar
4 tablespoons cilantro, chopped
4 tablespoons pickled ginger, minced
2 tablespoons pickled jalapeños,

minced   shelled and butterflied
4 teaspoons honey   4 teaspoons cornstarch
4 teaspoons sesame oil   1 cup water
3-4 garlic cloves, coarsely chopped   4 scallion flowers
Twenty 16-20 count shrimp, cleaned,   1 red bell pepper, finely julienne

To make the Scallion Risotto
1. Sauté the onion, scallions, and garlic in olive oil until the onions are soft.
2. Add the rice and sauté 3 minutes.
3. Reduce heat and add 1/2 cup of hot stock, continually adding it as the stock evaporates until all of the stock is used and the rice is tender.
4. Season with the pepper. (NOTE: Cooking the risotto too fast will make it crunchy; cooking it too slow will make it mushy.)

For the shrimp
1. Mix the vinegar, cilantro, ginger, jalapeños, and honey in a small bowl.
2. Heat the sesame oil in a heavy sauté pan.
3. Add the garlic and sauté 1-2 minutes.
4. Add the ginger mixture and the shrimp to the pan. Simmer until the shrimp are just cooked.
5. Dissolve the cornstarch in the water (put it in jar and shake vigorously).
6. Add the starch/water mixture to the sauté pan and continue to simmer until the sauce has thickened.

Scallion flowers
Cut each green onion 4" in length, then vertically into eighths 3/4 of the way down. Place in ice water so they will naturally "flare" open and stay crisp, for two hours.

1. Place the risotto on a large platter.
2. Arrange the shrimp on the risotto, and pour the sauce over all.
3. Place the scallion flowers evenly around the shrimp.
4. Sprinkle the slivered peppers over the shrimp and scallion flowers.

The wine with this recipe
…excellently dovetails into the food. The ginger, onion and spices in the dish are deliciously elevated by the wine, and its fruit flavors in turn are remarkably amplified.

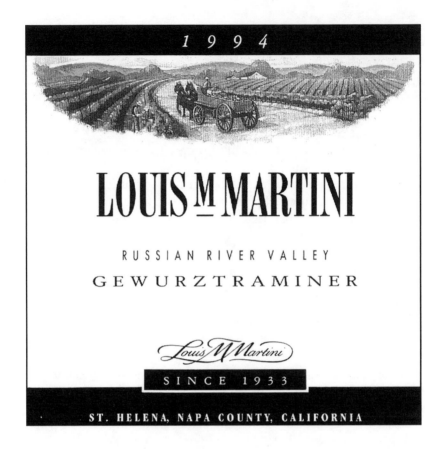

LOUIS M. MARTINI GEWÜRZTRAMINER

…is light gold in color, with an inviting floral nose and crisp tones. On the delicate side, there are excellent hints of spice in the well-balanced fruit. The good mouth-feel leads to a pleasing finish. A completely satisfying, drinkable wine.

SERVE WITH
ROASTED CORNISH GAME HENS

If you're interested in breaking away from the turkey rut at holiday times, or are just in the mood to have your palate tickled in a most appealing way, this is a wonderful approach. The magic that a touch of cardamom brings to this stuffing, along with the orange peel, dates, and pecans, marries with the slight gamishness of the hens and the spiced nature of the wine to create a meal beyond the ken of any American pilgrim. This triumph comes from Elizabeth Martini, and is truly worth giving thanks for. (6 servings)

STUFFING
2 cups chicken stock
1/2 teaspoon salt
1 tablespoon butter
1/4 teaspoon ground cinnamon
1/4 teaspoon ground cardamom
1 teaspoon freshly grated orange rind
1 cup long grain white rice

1/2 cup chopped pitted dates
1/2 cup chopped pecans

6 Cornish game hens
Salt, pepper
6 tablespoons butter, softened
1/2 cup orange marmalade
1/4 cup Gewürztraminer (Martini)

TO MAKE STUFFING
1. Add to the chicken stock the salt, butter, cinnamon, cardamom, and orange rind, and bring to a boil.
2. Add the rice, cover, and reduce heat. Simmer 20 minutes, then take off heat and allow to rest for 5 minutes.
3. Fluff the cooked rice with a fork, and stir in the dates and pecans.

FOR THE HENS
1. Pre-heat oven to 350°F.
2. Rinse the game hens and pat dry.
3. Salt and pepper the cavities and stuff with 1/2+ cup of rice apiece.
4. Secure legs with kitchen string, and place the hens in a roasting pan.
5. Brush the hens with the butter and begin roasting them in the oven.
6. Melt the orange marmalade with the wine and reduce slightly.
7. After 30 minutes, baste the hens with the marmalade mixture, raise the temperature to 400°F, and continue cooking for an additional 20-30 minutes, or until the juices run clear and the hens are browned, basting occasionally with the marmalade sauce. If the hens start to darken too much, cover with aluminum foil.

THE WINE WITH THIS RECIPE
…has its spices activated, and becomes even more fruity and smooth. Neither the wine nor the meal are too heavy, as the sweetness in the wine finds new life with the use of the cardomom. A gratifying pairing.

S P A R K L I N G

*T*HERE IS SOMETHING obvious as to why Champagne is regarded as something particularly appropriate for special occasions—it is special! The time and effort that go into making Champagne, with its many steps, sometimes quite complicated, produces wine imbued with sparkle and life. It has been said there is one wine that can be served throughout an entire meal, from salad and soup through entree (no matter what) to dessert, and that wine is Champagne.

The finest Champagnes are produced via the Méthode Champenoise. Put succinctly, it involves putting hermetically-sealed bottled wine through a second fermentation in a calm, cold, humid environment, letting it mature for three-to-five years, then finishing with remuage, dégorgement, and almost always a dosage (the finishing touch that affects the range of dryness). Such Champagnes will always proudly say on their labels Méthode Champenoise and sometimes also "Fermented in this bottle." If they don't, they're second class.

The discovery of Champagne is

wrapped in just enough shrouds of antiquity to allow two rival French houses to claim that right, Moët et Chandon and Taittinger. The former claims Dom Perignon, during his years as winemaker at the Abbey of Hautvillers, experimentally trapped the otherwise-allowed-to-escape carbon dioxide during the second fermentation of a batch of wine, and upon first taste professed "I am drinking stars!"; Taittinger claims its proprietary winemaster Dom Oudard achieved the same effect during the same period.

The Champagne history in the United States began in 1842 in Ohio, when one Nicholas Longworth created a sparkling wine from native Catawba grapes, but being *vitus labrusca* instead of the more appropriate *vitus vinifera*, it lacked the subtlety of its European counterpart. California began its production quite slowly, starting in 1855 in the San Gabriel area in Southern California, when Benjamin Davis Wilson (for whom Mt. Wilson is named) produced a sparkling wine from Mission grapes. Northern California began two years later near San Jose, thanks to brothers Jean-Louis and Pierre Sainsevain, and by the following year produced 150,000 cases. The venerable General Maricio Vallejo also tried his hand in 1859. However, none of these pioneer

California champagne ventures lasted long.

The Haraszthys, Agoston and son Arpad, made the strongest push via their Buena Vista winery, but a combination of the inappropriate Mission grapes and technical shortcomings (and misunderstandings of the Champagne process) led to a disaster. But, in time, with French Champagne master Pierre Debanne from the defunct frères Sainsevain operation, they got out a more consistent product. Meanwhile, Arpad split off on his own and began producing sparkling wine with such grapes as Riesling, Burger, Gutedel, Muscatel, and Zinfandel. In fact, his cuvée dubbed "Dry Eclipse" became somewhat of a national success. During this same period (1875-85), other houses were founded and produced high-quality sparkling wines, such as Korbel, Almaden and Paul Masson.

Although some success was obtained in the ensuing decades, the ridiculous social experiment that was Prohibition smothered the Champagne industry through the 1920s, save for a few limited-use allowances that permitted Paul Masson and others to produce a fractionable amount during this period. Upon the repeal of the Volstead Act in 1933, the restart was choppy and slow in developing. The California Champagne industry was given a temporary boost by World War II (caused by the virtual cessation of French imports), and has gone on to become the second largest Champagne and sparkling wine producer in the world.

Although bulk wine producers lionized the American Champagne market during the post-war years, producers such as Korbel, Hans Kornell, and Martin Ray stuck with the purist Méthode Champenoise. The next wave of devotees to produce Champagne of distinction began in the mid-to-late 1960s, when Jack and Jamie Davies revived Schramsberg and began a virtual revolution in Champagne excellence in California. When President Nixon toasted Premier Chou En-lai in the Great Hall of the People in the People's Republic of China in 1972, it was with Schramsberg 1969 Blanc de Blancs. The world, and France, paid attention.

Sensing California was the place to be, many French Champagne houses began to establish affiliated Champagneries there, including Moët, Mumm, Taittinger, Roederer, Deutz, and Piper-Heidsieck. Soon to follow were the Spanish firms of Codorniu and Freixenet. Several domestic wineries also began to establish themselves as quality Champagne forces to be reckoned with, such as Iron Horse, S. Anderson and Jordan.

The varieties used in California are those typically found in Champagne: Chardonnay, Pinot Noir, and to a much lesser extent Pinot Meunier. That's not to say other grapes can't be used. For example, one grape, the hybrid "Flora" (a genetic cross between Semillon and Gewürztraminer) developed at the UC-Davis School of Enology, is used by Schramsberg in their pétillant Crémant with delicious success.

A sticking point regarding product nomenclature continues to fester and pester: Champagne in France is entirely proprietary, sparkling wine made anywhere else in that country barred from labeling itself Champagne. Taking it further, the French wine industry has attempted to make this an international standard, so that no one anywhere in the world should call their sparklers "Champagne," and for the most part successfully so. However, since the United States government established its regulations a century prior, American consumers have been thoroughly enculturated into accepting the word Champagne as representing sparkling wine of all types regardless of origin. With marketing and competition such as it is, only a few American producers have agreed to the French request. For some, it's an issue of great concern; for others, it's a tempest in a wine flute.

So whether you're celebrating a special moment in life or are just happy to still be breathing, Champagne is the perfect wine for all occasions. And if it's not a spur-of-the-moment occasion but a thoughtful and maybe even grand occasion (and "happy to still be breathing" certainly qualifies), there are several suggestions that follow!

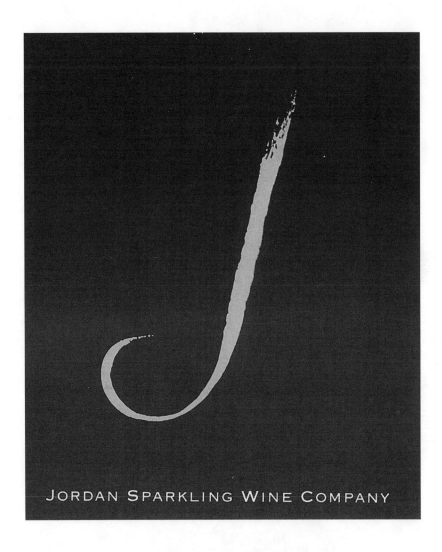

JORDAN SPARKLING WINE COMPANY

"J", JORDAN SPARKLING WINE

…is elegant looking in the glass. Nice golden color with refined bubbles, it possesses a yeasty yet soft nose with a hint of fruit. Good feel in the mouth with a pleasant dryness and a smooth, creamy finish. Well-balanced and flavorful.

SERVE WITH
Tuna Tartare

This dish is a simple, sushi-like appetizer, in which the edge of raw fish is "cooked" by the acids in the lemon and vinegar, and comes from the chefs at Jordan Winery. (8 servings)

$1^1/4$ pounds very fresh ahi tuna
1 tablespoon each chives, cilantro, and dill, chopped
$1^1/2$ tablespoons lemon juice
$1^1/2$ tablespoons white wine vinegar
2 tablespoons extra virgin olive oil (on the lighter side is best)
Salt and fresh ground black pepper.
Garnish
Radicchio or butter lettuce
1 hard boiled egg, pressed through a fine sieve
Vinaigrette
3 tablespoons lemon juice
9 tablespoons olive oil

To prepare Tartare
Chop tuna into $1/4$" dice.
Combine with herbs, lemon juice, and olive oil. Season with salt and
   pepper to taste.
Chill for at least one hour before serving.
To serve
Place a serving of tuna tartare on a radicchio or butter lettuce leaf.
Sprinkle the ball of tartare with chopped egg.
Spoon a little vinaigrette around the leaf.

The wine with this recipe
...certainly brings out the flavor of the food. The sparkler becomes more round and full, the fruit is a bit more prevalent, and the character livelier. An ideal accompaniment!

DOMAINE CHANDON BRUT RÉSERVE

...has a medium golden color, the nose presenting alluring scents of apricot and pear, and the fruit of the vine. The reserved quality of the yeast scent makes for a crisper sensation, very appealing. Quite dry in the mouth, it releases its fruit with a full heart, then creates a fresh and creamy feel as it finishes, a lasting impression full of wonder and marvel.

SERVE WITH

EGGPLANT, ZUCCHINI AND TOMATO "TARTE TATIN"

This recipe, from the master touch of Philippe Jeanty, Executive Chef at the Champagnery, creates mini-tartes that are cooked with the "crust" on top and served upside-down. This makes for a substantial hors d'oeuvres or can serve as a magnificent part of an all-Champagne meal. Different effects can be expected from each of the squashes, so you may have to try them all! (6 servings)

1 medium-large squash—acorn, butternut or pumpkin
4 medium zucchini
4 tomatoes
5-6 Japanese eggplants
Olive oil
Herb de Provence:
   $1/2$ teaspoon each rosemary, thyme, and lavender or sage
2 tablespoons sweet butter
Frozen puff pastry
Fresh chervil leaves
Six 4" tart pans

1. Peel the squash, cut in half, scrape out the seeds, and slice into eighths. Cut both ends of the zucchinis, cut in half lengthwise, and slice into eighths on a mandoline. Slice tomatoes across, then cut slices in half. Cut the eggplant by hand on a bias, then toss in pure olive oil. Keep all ingredients separate.
2. Line the bottom of six 4" tart pans with parchment paper cut in circles; butter the sides of the pans, then season bottoms with Herb de Provence.
3. Alternate layers of each vegetable across tart pan, packing them tightly, then packing them some more. Season each tarte tatin with salt, pepper, and more Herb de Provence. Drizzle tops with olive oil, and little pieces of whole sweet butter.
4. Bake tartes in 500°F oven for 12 minutes, remove.
Quickly cover each with a prepared $4^1/2$" circle of puff pastry, tuck in edges if necessary, return tartes to the oven, and bake an additional 4-6 minutes at 400°F.
5. Remove from oven, let slightly cool, then turn tartes upside-down on individual serving plates, garnish with fresh chervil leaves, and serve.

THE WINE WITH THIS RECIPE

...spreads out its richness and becomes enlivened by the encounter. The subtleties that are a part of the soft-toned vegetables, highlighted by the herbs, create a glorious labyrinth of flavors in combination with the wine that are intriguing, enticing and captivating. This is worth savoring slowly, as the taste sensations playfully dawdle and stretch, clearly in no hurry to dissipate and disappear.

DOMAINE CHANDON ÉTOILE

…is delicate, a light golden color with refined bubbles. Clearly French in style, there are quiet floral hints in the nose, hints of fruit, of yeast, subtle but present. As promised, the taste is clean but full, rich in its elements, confident and aristrocratic.

CHEESECAKE WITH STRAWBERRIES MARINATED IN SPARKLING WINE

This scintillating dessert is the creation of Domain Chandon's Executive Chef Philippe Jeanty. A crustless cheesecake, it relies on a foil-lined springform pan, and is baked not unlike a custard. (8 servings)

1 1/2 pounds cream cheese, room temperature
4 eggs
3/4 cup sugar
1 cup sour cream
1 teaspoon vanilla
Zest of half a lemon

Strawberry Sauce & Marinated Strawberries
2 pint-size baskets of strawberries
1/2 bottle Champagne (Domaine Chandon étoile or Blanc de Noirs)
1/2 cup sugar

TO MAKE CHEESECAKE
1. Blend cream cheese, eggs, sugar, sour cream, vanilla and lemon zest with an electric mixer for 30 minutes.
2. Line 9" springform pan with aluminum foil, making sure it is watertight. Pour in the mixture. Place cake pan in larger pan, then fill it with enough warm water to surround the lower half of the cake pan. Bake for 45 minutes at 325°F.
3. Remove pans from the oven, remove cake from water, and let cool either to room temperature or in refrigerator.

TO MAKE SAUCE AND STRAWBERRIES
1. In a saucepan, cook one basket of strawberries with 1/4 cup sugar over medium heat for about 10 minutes, then blend and cool.
2. Marinate the second basket of strawberries in the sparkling wine and 1/4 cup sugar for 2 hours.

Serve slices of the cheesecake garnished with a spoonful of the marinated strawberries and a spoonful of the sauce.

THE WINE WITH THIS RECIPE
...becomes livelier and much creamier, as hints of sweetness emerge with charm and breeding. The fruit in the wine responds well with both the strawberries and its sauce, and rounds out in the mouth with a satisfying Champagne feel. There is grace.

IRON HORSE BRUT

...features a medium-light golden color, releasing beautiful yeast and fruit in the nose, with touches of apricot. Appealing and lively in the glass. Clearly rich and complex in the mouth, a virtual flavor explosion, hints of nuttiness, pecans. The bubbles literally texturize the tongue—a most compelling experience, so that one wants more and more!

SERVE WITH
ROAST CHICKEN WITH LEMON AND OLIVES

This recipe, which comes from the winery itself, asks for a roasting chicken that is special to the Sonoma County area. Although "Rocky the Free-Range Chicken" sounds like it could be a cartoon character, these birds, either in Junior or Senior sizes, are clearly not pen-fed or force-fed, but allowed to consume that which nature provides. They are now available throughout the state of California and in various areas of the United States in the more gourmet-oriented grocery stores. (4 servings)

1 4¹/2-pound free-range roasting chicken, preferably "Rocky"
Salt and pepper, to taste
1 bunch thyme
2 lemons, cut in half
1 tablespoon olive oil
1 cup of olives (nicoise, kalamata, or picholine), pitted

1. Preheat oven to 450°F.
2. Wash chicken inside and out, and dry thoroughly. Season cavity with salt and pepper. Place the thyme and lemon halves inside the chicken, and rub the bird entirely with olive oil.
3. Truss the chicken, set it breast side down on a roasting pan, and place it on upper rack of oven. Cook for 45 minutes, then turn breast side up, lower heat to 350°F, and cook for an additional 15 minutes, basting with cooking juices.
4. When done (juice runs clear), remove from oven, let sit for a few minutes, then carve and serve with savory juices on top, scattering olives over and around the platter.

THE WINE WITH THIS RECIPE

...becomes almost robust! The yeastiness emerges beautifully, and accents of citrus flash off the lemon with bright clarity. The bubbles hold up nicely with the food, and help to increase the depth and range of the flavors as they interact. With the touch of olives adding a Mediterranean quality to the mix, the complexity grows in attractiveness and becomes completely satisfying.

ESTATE   BOTTLED

IRON HORSE™
BRUT ROSÉ
SPARKLING WINE, SONOMA COUNTY GREEN VALLEY

ALC. 13.0% VOL.   NET VOL. 750 ML.

1991

IRON HORSE BRUT ROSÉ

...enjoys a deep salmon hue, and contributes a lovely, delicate nose with a slight nod of yeast, tight and pleasing. There is a lovely softness in the mouth, full and attractively bold, fresh tasting. There is a flash of sweetness that quickly dissipates into a clean feel and a dry finish that seems to perpetuate itself. With its precise, elegant bubbles, this is a delicious, great drinking sparkler.

SERVE WITH
CHARCOAL-GRILLED ROCKFISH
WITH GREEN ONION AND TOMATO RELISH

A gloriously simple to prepare yet savory recipe, colorful as can be. This comes from Mark Malicki, chef for the winery. If rockfish as such are unavailable, substitute Pacific red snapper filets or perch. You might even find it's easier to buy a plant of lemon verbena at a nursery than finding any in stores; your herb garden benefits, its useful in this and other recipes, and it also makes a very soothing tea. (4 servings)

4 cloves garlic, peeled
1 small bunch of lemon verbena
Salt & pepper
3 cups olive oil
12 small rockfish (1 pound), such as Golden Eye, Scarlet Ruby, etc.
1 bunch green onions, chopped
2 pounds ripe tomatoes, peeled, seeded, and chopped

1. In a mortar or molcajete, pound together the garlic, lemon verbena, and salt and pepper into a paste. Add 2/3 of the olive oil; put in a bowl, add the fish, and marinate for 30 minutes.
2. Mix the green onions and tomatoes together with the remainder of the oil, add salt and pepper, and let marry.
3. Place fish on a medium-hot grill; cook 5 minutes on each side. Serve with the relish.

THE WINE WITH THE RECIPE
…gains a whole new perspective. The olive oil/green onion/tomato flavors bring a seductive smoothness to the wine, and the fruit and flavors of the wine are amplified by the process. It blossoms and is clearly enhanced by the combination. Flavorful, colorful, carefree and substantial at the same time, this is a most engaging get-together.

ESTATE   BOTTLED

IRON HORSE
WEDDING CUVÉE
SPARKLING WINE, SONOMA COUNTY GREEN VALLEY

ALC. 12.5% VOL.   NET VOL. 750 ML.

1993

IRON HORSE WEDDING CUVÉE

...has a clear light salmon tint, sharply defined bubbles, and releases an aroma with slight hints of yeast and fruit, very clean. In the mouth, the full flavors of Champagne are released, full fruit, balanced, and a lasting finish. One of the best sparkling wines produced in California, bar none.

Serve with
SALMON AND SCALLOP CARPACCIO

This is a light, bright salad, that is simple to prepare and quite lovely in presentation. The raw concern of the salmon is thoroughly muted by its paper-thinness and the flavor of the scallops, which get a dash of citrus-flavor from the herby verbena. A creation of winery chef Mark Malicki, this is an ethereal beginning to any meal. (4 servings)

FOR THE SALMON
4 1 ounce slices of salmon, $1/2$" thick
8 8" square pieces of clear wrap

FOR THE SCALLOPS
4 large sea scallops
1 bunch lemon verbena
2 cups water

DRESSING
1 shallot, finely chopped

Juice of 1 lemon
8 teaspoons extra virgin olive oil

FOR THE GREENS
$1/2$ pound mixed greens, such as
   mizuna, arugula, watercress,
   borage, mint, orach, amaranth, etc.
4 teaspoons sparkling wine
Kosher salt
Cracked pepper

SALMON

Place a slice of salmon between two sheets of wrap. With a cleaver or, even better, a tortilla press, gently flatten until the salmon gives the appearance of being translucent. (With the press, its possible to adjust the salmon and even fold portions back over for additional presses in order to achieve a less haphazard shape when done.) Repeat the process with the rest of the salmon. Place in the refrigerator.

SCALLOPS

1. Bring 2 cups of water to boil; add 1 bunch lemon verbena. Turn off water and let steep for 30 minutes.
2. Remove the herb, bring water back to a simmer, then plunge scallops in liquid for 30-45 seconds or until they just turn opaque. Immediately remove cooked scallops and place in ice water.
3. When cooled, slice scallops against the grain into paper-thin slices, and refrigerate.

DRESSING

Mince shallots. Add lemon juice and olive oil. Let stand for 15 minutes.

FINAL PREPARATION

1. Place greens in a bowl and toss with sparkling wine, then season with salt and pepper to taste. Evenly distribute greens on four chilled salad plates.
2. Partially cover greens with slice of salmon on top; decoratively arrange equal portions of sliced scallops on salmon.
3. Drizzle dressing over all, and serve.

THE WINE WITH THIS RECIPE

...has its flavors increased all the more. The acids in the greens accent the acid in the wine perfectly, and the contrasts in flavors continue to amaze, bringing fresh aspects every second. The smoothness of the scallops and the easy salmon flavors meld nicely, and burst into the wine, causing the effervesence to become almost pyrotechnical, even involving the lips!

S. ANDERSON BRUT

...displays a nice golden color, light in style but not in substance, as its flashing tiny bubbles promise. It has a solid, fruity nose, with clean yeast expression, a crisp smelling, obviously superior sparkler. It has a secure feel in the mouth, opens up its fruit, is a bit buffered by a lovely, soft creaminess, and exhibits good acid balance. The finish floats along, maintaining the levels of complexities well.

SERVE WITH
PRAWNS WITH CHAMPAGNE BUTTER

An appetizer or part of a main course, this dish is embellished with the extra splash of flavor from the anchovy paste and sage, which admirably creates more delicacy and savor. A fun and flavorful way to make shrimp, this was the inspiration of Tracy W. Anderson. (4-6 servings)

1 pound large prawns, shelled and de-veined
1/2 pound sliced bacon
1/4 cup champagne (S. Anderson)
1 stick butter, cut into pieces
1/4 teaspoon anchovy paste
2 garlic cloves, minced
2 teaspoons chopped fresh sage leaves

1. Wrap each prawn with bacon—this will take 1/3-1/2 piece of bacon per prawn. With two long skewers that have been soaked in water to better withstand the heat of the fire, use one to skewer the tail end of 4 prawns, then parallel this with the other skewer through the head end, creating almost a "railroad" effect, the skewers the rails, the shrimp the ties. Leave a little space between each prawn so the bacon can cook all around. (You don't have to skewer them at all, but they tend to curl if you don't, and they're easier to flip over during cooking.) Set aside while you make the butter sauce.
2. To make the basting sauce, put the champagne in a small saucepan and bring to a boil. Reduce slightly over medium heat, then turn off the flame and add the butter, whisking to combine. Add the anchovy paste, garlic, and sage. Keep warm, but do not boil again.
3. Grill the shrimp over coals (not too long) basting with the butter sauce until the bacon is brown and the shrimp are cooked through. (You can sauté them in a frying pan over medium-high heat; do not add oil to the pan—the bacon grease will suffice—and also do not baste them with the sauce while cooking, but use when serving.)
4. Place the cooked shrimp on a serving platter. Remove the skewers, coat lavishly with the butter sauce and serve.

THE WINE WITH THIS RECIPE
...gets a boost from the lovely smokiness that comes from the bacon and the process, making it a richer, substantial experience. The sage makes a solid hit with the fruit, adding an unforeseen depth. The wine's noble character is wonderfully enhanced by this dish.

BLANC DE NOIRS

NAPA VALLEY
CHAMPAGNE

VINTAGE 1988

PRODUCED AND BOTTLED BY SCHRAMSBERG VINEYARDS·CALISTOGA CALIFORNIA
ALCOHOL 12% BY VOLUME   CONTENTS 750 MLS

SCHRAMSBERG BLANC DE NOIRS

...*is straw-tinged in color, with microscopic bubbles and a healthy dose of yeast in the nose. It is supremely dry in the mouth, releasing essences of peach and apricot, smooth and full, with a touch of creaminess. The acid provides a slight, pleasing edge, a brightness along with the yeast. The finish maintains the flavors for a pleasing, well-served close.*

SERVE WITH
SEA BASS IN PARCHMENT WITH LEEKS AND GINGER

Great things come in small packages! This baked-in-a-pouch fish entree is lightly savory and also makes for a fun presentation at table. Jamie Davies, co-owner of the Champagnery, is nothing short of prolific at creating remarkable dishes to go with their spectacular sparklings, and this is no exception. (6 servings)

3-4 medium-size leeks
6 tablespoons butter
3 slices fresh ginger root, cut into thin julienne
$1/2$ cup Schramsberg Blanc de Noirs Champagne
2 carrots, cut into julienne
1 red bell pepper, cut into julienne
3 green onion tops, cut into julienne
Salt and freshly ground black pepper, to taste
6 sea bass fillets (4 ounce filets cut 1" thick)

1. Split leeks lengthwise, wash well under cold running water, and cut white part and some of the green into short, thin julienne.
2. In a skillet, melt butter and sauté leeks until thoroughly wilted, about 5 minutes. Add ginger and Champagne. Cook briskly until liquid evaporates. Remove from the heat and set aside to cool.
3. Cut cooking parchment into 16"-by-24" pieces. Fold each piece in half crosswise and cut out to form heart shape. Open hearts flat and place one-sixth of the leek mixture on one-half of each heart, leaving a 1" border. Top with one-sixth of the carrots, bell pepper, and onion tops. Place a fish fillet on top of each portion of vegetables. Season lightly with salt and pepper.
4. Fold heart over fish and form a series of small pleats around open side, pressing sharply and folding up to seal edges together. Place packets on baking sheets.
5. Bake in a preheated 400°F oven for 5-6 minutes, or until packets puff and start to brown. Serve at once; let guests open packets at the table.

THE WINE WITH THIS RECIPE
…is considerably fruitier and brighter, and actually becomes more beneficially sec. The mild onion qualities of the leeks and scallions, blended with the bell pepper, provide a springboard for the yeast to expand and contribute, and the zing from the ginger intensifies the fruit. With the smooth taste and texture of the bass meshing with the creamy quality of the wine, producing a full and flavorful finish, the total effect is extremely pleasurable and provoking.

BRUT ROSÉ

NAPA VALLEY   VINTAGE 1991
CHAMPAGNE   CUVÉE DE PINOT

PRODUCED AND BOTTLED BY SCHRAMSBERG VINEYARDS·CALISTOGA CALIFORNIA
ALCOHOL 12% BY VOLUME   CONTENTS 750 MLS

SCHRAMSBERG BRUT ROSÉ (CUVÉE DE PINOT)

...features a beautiful salmon hue, and a nose that releases solid yeast character and a wealth of fruit, simply one of the nicest smelling sparklers made. The bubbles are joyously fine, delicate, pinpoint, a key indication of Champenoise excellence. The body enjoys excellent fruit and acid balance, its slight creaminess guiding it well. The mouth feel is pure effervesence, as it actively surrounds the palate and heightens the senses. A gorgeous experience, inside and out!

SERVE WITH
MUSHROOM TART

A mushroom custard pie that is subtle, flavorful, and pleasing to the eye, which is also an accurate description of its wine match! Jamie Davies, co-owner of the winery, is masterful at detecting those flavors in food that coordinate with their wines. (8 servings)

Partially baked quiche shell
6 slices bacon, finely diced
3 tablespoons olive oil
1 pound mushrooms (a combination of wild and domestic), thinly sliced
2 cloves garlic
2 tablespoons parsley, finely minced
1/2 teaspoon dried tarragon, crumbled
4 eggs
1 cup milk or half-and-half
1 cup fresh grated Parmesan or Asiago cheese
1/4 teaspoon each salt and freshly ground pepper

1. Prepare quiche shell, using standard recipe. Bake per recipe's directed oven temperature, crust lip covered with a ring of foil, for 20 minutes or until just beginning to brown.
2. In a large skillet, cook bacon until crisp; remove from pan with a slotted utensil and drain on paper towels. Pour out bacon drippings but leave residue.
3. In same skillet, heat the oil and sauté mushrooms until soft, about 2 minutes. Add garlic, parsley, and tarragon, and remove from heat; cool to room temperature.
4. Beat eggs until light, then stir in milk, the cooled mushroom mixture, cheese, reserved bacon, salt, and pepper. Pour into prepared quiche shell.
5. Bake in a pre-heated 350°F oven for 25-40 minutes, or until set, using a toothpick to check for doneness. Cool on rack. Serve warm or at room temperature.

THE WINE WITH THIS RECIPE

…has its fruit tones deliciously amplified. The smokiness of the bacon lends a rustic quality to the wine, modifying the yeast aspects to create a freshness and solid feel in the mouth. The dish unreservedly complements the wine, which in turn highlights the warmth and substance of the pie.

Schramsberg
FOUNDED 1862 ®

NAPA VALLEY
CRÉMANT

DEMI-SEC   VINTAGE 1992

PRODUCED AND BOTTLED BY SCHRAMSBERG VINEYARDS·CALISTOGA CALIFORNIA
ALCOHOL 12% BY VOLUME   CONTENTS 750 MLS

SCHRAMSBERG CRÉMANT

…exhibits a light, golden color and petite bubbles. The allure of the Flora grape that is the basis of this wine comes through in the nose, with pleasant hints of yeast emerging from the sweet overtones. It offers a rich feel in the mouth, a softened floral quality that offers apricot and nectarine, and hints at sweetness with a delicate touch that evolves into a thorough creaminess in the finish.

SERVE WITH
NECTARINE TART

This is an easy and colorful dessert created by Jamie Davies, co-owner of the winery, one that looks as impressive as it tastes. Fruit flavors from the nectarines, peach preserves, raspberries, orange zest, and orange liqueur, accent the creaminess of the sparkling wine. (6-8 servings)

ALMOND TART SHELL
2 ounces slivered almonds
   (about 1/2 cup)
1 cup all-purpose flour
1/4 cup sugar
3 spiral pieces orange zest
1 teaspoon ground mace
10 tablespoons cold unsalted

butter, cut up
1 egg
NECTARINE FILLING
1 3/4 pounds nectarines, halved,
   pitted, and peeled, if desired
1/3 cup sugar
3 tablespoons unsalted butter
2 tablespoons orange liqueur

GLAZE
1/2 cup peach preserves, sieved

2 tablespoons orange liqueur
Fresh raspberries for garnish

TO MAKE ALMOND TART SHELL
1. In food processor, process almonds until reduced to fine powder. Add flour, sugar, orange zest, and mace. Process until zest is in fine pieces.
2. Add 10 tablespoons butter. Pulse with on/off turns until evenly crumbly.
3. Add egg. Process until mixture pulls away from sides of bowl and forms a ball. Shape dough into a disk. Wrap and refrigerate 1 hour.
4. Flour top and bottom of dough. Roll out between 2 pieces of well-floured waxed paper.
5. Remove top sheet of waxed paper. Invert pastry over 9" tart pan with removable bottom. Carefully peel off waxed paper. The pastry is delicate and tears easily, but it is easily mended by patching and pressing the pieces together. Trim dough even with edge.
6. Place on baking sheet. Freeze while preparing filling.

TO MAKE NECTARINE FILLING
1. Preheat oven to 400°F.
2. Cut nectarine halves in thin slices, keeping halves intact. In pastry shell, fan out nectarine slices in pinwheel design.
3. Sprinkle nectarines with 1/3 cup sugar. Dot with 3 tablespoons butter. Drizzle with 2 tablespoons orange liqueur.
4. Bake tart on baking sheet for 50 to 60 minutes until sugar caramelizes and juices bubble in center of tart.
5. Cool on rack 20 minutes before glazing.

TO GLAZE AND COMPLETE DISH
1. While tart is cooling, in a small bowl, combine sieved preserves and 2 tablespoons orange liqueur. Mix well.
2. Spoon evenly over warm nectarines to glaze. Garnish with raspberries.

THE WINE WITH THIS RECIPE
…is at one with the universe. The nuttiness in the tart elicits incredible nuances in the wine, with the creaminess emerging to an even finer degree. The fruit in the tart is clearly found in the wine, and the trace of orange liqueur in the dish brings out a flash of crispness in the Champagne that adds to its complexities.

PINOT NOIR

*P*INOT NOIR is recognized as perhaps the world's most difficult wine to produce qualitatively—on the average, only one out of three vintages are deemed exceptional in Burgundy, its French home of origin. Variables abound: Soil, climate, frosts, quantity of fruit, clone-type (there are hundreds), which means every year, every vintage, can be remarkably different—in France. Fortunately for us, California presents a slightly more stable weather environment, which makes the quality of grapes a bit more consistent.

First introduced into California in 1885 at the California Agricultural Experiment Station, Pinot Noir was not originally thought to be well-suited for the state. However, over the years, certain areas of California have proven to be more than adequate, such as Carneros, the Lower Russian River, Green Valley, the Santa Cruz Mountains, and Pinnacles (where Calera and Chalone have had considerable success); of late, one area in particular seems to incorporate the much sought-after balance of climate and chalky limestone soil deemed best for Pinot Noir: the Central Coast area of Santa Barbara and San Luis Obispo Counties, which produce some phenomenally brilliant wines; it is conceded that the above areas are generally regarded as prime territories in the state.

As implied, Pinot Noir seems to have done best in California where planted in microclimates similar to Burgundy. This reflects a desire—at times, an obsession—to secure a California version of Burgundy's "terroir," which might be loosely defined as the sum total of soil/ earth/air/moisture/ambient influences thus being mystically greater than its parts, as it affects the vines, the grapes, and the resulting wine. In simpler terms, if all the pieces are assembled correctly, wonderful wines get made, and California is doing it.

Pinot Noir is not often crafted to age for extended periods, 5-7 years being the usual life expectancy, but like any fine red wine it will improve over time when given the chance— for just how long is a matter of individual advice, interpretation of wine composition, and your ability to avoid temptation!

Certainly, the wines that follow have developed their own sense of terroir, and the accompanying recipes will enhance them even more.

ACACIA PINOT NOIR
RESERVE CARNEROS

...features a medium-light, red/purple color, and delivers an excellently earthy Pinot Noir nose, with full inviting fruit. It has a great mouth feel, a bit silky along with its spice and light pepper, with up-front fruitiness and outstanding balance. With its deep, dark fruit flavors, a subtle yet apparent earthiness, it delivers a voluptuous finish, and altogether is resoundingly engaging.

SERVE WITH
GRILLED SMALL BIRDS

This recipe was especially crafted by Susan Brooks, wife of winemaker Larry, for this wine. Noting Pinot Noir's affinity for smoked and grilled foods, she matched it with the mildly hearty flavors that can be found in game birds, from meaty Cornish game hens to delicate quail to dark-meat squab. She advises that you should be a bit more lenient with the herbs and spices with older vintages of the wine, which is why the amounts in the recipe vary. (This wine was similarly matched with barbecued pheasant with outstanding results.)

1-2 small game birds per person
  (Cornish game hens, quail, squab, partridge, grouse)
2-6 tablespoons olive oil
1-3 tablespoons fresh herbs (rosemary, thyme)
1-3 cloves garlic, minced
1-3 teaspoons lemon rind, grated
1-2 teaspoons fresh ginger, grated

1. Wash the birds well in cold water, and pat dry.
2. Cut larger birds in half lengthwise through the breast, leaving the smallish quail whole, then thoroughly salt and pepper.
3. Create a marinade from the oil, herbs, garlic, lemon rind and ginger.
4. In a glass or ceramic pan, mix the birds and the marinade, and place in the refrigerator for up to 6 hours. (Plastic freezer bags are too readily punctured by the sharp wing ends of these fowl.)
5. When time to cook, place the birds on a barbecue grill skin side down and cook 5-8 minutes per side, depending on the heat of the fire, the size of the bird, and desired doneness. (You might want to start the larger birds first, then follow with the smaller, more quick-to-cook others.)

THE WINE WITH THIS RECIPE

…becomes different with each type of bird, and exemplifies the fun and beauty of taste combinations. Tested with Cornish game hens, squab and quail, they and the marinade worked to bring out the delightful spiciness in the wine. The game hens were extremely complementary, with an intriguing gaminess that heightened the wine's fruitiness; the squab contained an inherent spice that, along with the wine's, further activated a gorgeous earthiness, as well as punching up the fruit; and the quail created a brighter, lighter, and fruitier experience. As a sort of gamely smorgasbord offering, this is an engaging way to test the many values of wine and food pairing.

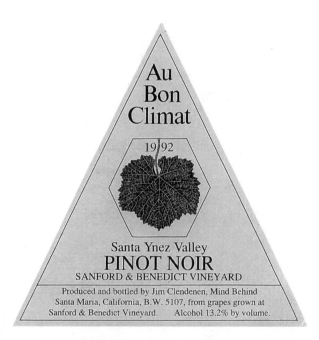

AU BON CLIMAT PINOT NOIR
SANFORD & BENEDICT

…is medium-red/purple in color, with an explosive nose, cherry, raspberry, earth, smoke, truly expressive. It further erupts in the mouth, bursting, deep raspberry, big in style while still clearly delicate with its well-crafted tannin structure. A lingering finish maintains this sense of control over its elements, and makes for an astounding California "Red Burgundy."

SERVE WITH
ROAST PRIME RIB WITH AU GRATIN POTATOES

A classic wine-and-beef combination, this favorite was adapted by Donna Oken, Santa Barbara wine involvee and culinary gem. It includes au gratin potatoes, which are an absolutely appropriate accompaniment for this hearty fare, and which can be cooked right along with the roast, as they both take the same oven temperature. (6-8 servings)

4-5 pounds prime rib of beef   **WHITE SAUCE**
Salt, cracked black pepper   4 tablespoons butter

4 tablespoons flour
1/4 teaspoon salt
1/4 teaspoon pepper
1 1/2 teaspoons dried herb medley
 (oregano, thyme, rosemary, sage)
2 1/4 cups milk

3 tablespoons butter
6 potatoes (russets or Yukon
 gold), pared and thinly sliced
Salt
2 yellow onions, thinly sliced
1/2-1 lb. grated cheddar cheese

FOR THE ROAST

1. Pre-heat oven to 500°F.
2. Place roast in a roasting pan, fat side up, and season with salt and cracked pepper.
3. Sear meat in oven for 15 minutes, then reduce temperature to 350°F and continue cooking until done: 20 minutes per pound for rare, 30 minutes per pound for medium.

FOR THE POTATOES

1. Melt 4 tablespoons of butter in a pot over low heat.
2. Blend in the flour, salt, pepper and herbs, and stir the roux while cooking 1 minute or until mixture becomes bubbly and smooth.
3. Remove pan from the heat, and add the milk, stirring thoroughly.
4. Return pan to stove and increase heat until a slight boil is produced; immediately reduce heat, and continue to simmer and stir for 10 minutes or until the sauce has thickened.
5. Completely grease a casserole dish with 3 tablespoons butter.
6. Spoon enough of the white sauce to cover the bottom of dish.
7. Make a thin layer of the potatoes on the sauce, lightly salt, then follow with a thin layer of sliced onions and 4-6 ounces of the grated cheese.
8. Repeat layers (sauce/potatoes/onions/cheese) until the potatoes and onion have been used, ending with a final topping of sauce.
9. Bake in 350°F oven for 75 minutes; sprinkle top with more grated cheese for the final 15 minutes of baking, if desired.

THE WINE WITH THE RECIPE

…has its components seemingly blossom to new contributions; the elegance and glory of the wine, its spiciness and earthy character, evolve into full statements of self. The light but rich flavors that make a prime rib so special, along with the touch of pepper, surge into the fruit in the wine and create music.

CALERA PINOT NOIR
JENSEN

...is medium-light, slightly brick in color, with enticing barnyard character in its big, bold nose—accents of pepper, with a glimpse of dark cherry. There is a full feel in the mouth as it explodes with fruit. The pepperiness is subtly infused throughout this well-rounded, expertly balanced wine. As it lingers in the mouth, a background of blackberry emerges through its light tannins. An honest sense of earthiness, a very complex, intriguing, glorious Pinot Noir.

SERVE WITH
SQUAB SALAD WITH SHERRY VINEGAR AND RED WINE SAUCE

Chef supreme Robert Grenner created this fresh angle on grilled poultry and salad. The squab stock-sauce serves as the "oil" part, and when combined with the pool of cayenne-influence vinegar completes the dressing. If you barbecue the wings and legs along with the breasts, you can serve them on the side as an extra nosh for those who can't get enough of this very good thing. (4-8 servings)

1/2 squab per person
Madiera
SQUAB STOCK
  Mirepoix
  Bouquet garni
  1 bottle red wine
  2 tablespoons minced garlic
1/4 cup Sherry vinegar

1/2 teaspoon cayenne pepper
1/2 teaspoon cornstarch
1 bunch mâche
4 arugula leaves
Daikon radish, finely julienne
Carrot, finely julienne
Cucumber, finely julienne

To prepare the squabs
1. Debone the squabs except for the legs, reserving carcass.
2. Marinate the squab meat and legs in Madiera 2 hours before grilling.

To make squab stock/sauce
1. Roast the squab bones and mirepoix in a 375°F oven for 20 minutes, turning occasionally.
2. Place the bones in a deep pan, add the bouquet garni, wine and garlic, bring to a boil, reduce heat, and reduce by 1/2.
3. Strain and reserve the stock.

For the vinegar sauce
1. Add cayenne to vinegar, thoroughly mix.
2. Place 1 tablespoon vinegar mix in jar.
3. Add cornstarch, cover, and shake until completely dissolved.
4. Add vinegar-cornstarch mix to rest of vinegar, combine.

To complete the dish
1. Grill the squab on medium-hot coals until done. Slice into strips.
2. Toss greens, radish, carrot and cucumber with cooked squab.
3. Add stock sauce, retoss.
4. Create a pool of vinegar sauce in the center of each salad plate.
5. Place individual servings of squab salad on top of pool, serve.

The wine with this recipe
…explodes with flavor, the spiciness of the dressing pairing up with the spiciness in the wine. The terroir of the wine enjoys the gaminess of the squab, and the fruit comes out full and hearty, including a flash of dark cherry. The greens, with the touch of arugula, enjoy the light tannins in the wine. There is great finesse with these flavors, and this match is quite an accomplishment.

1993
NAPA VALLEY
PINOT NOIR
RESERVE
UNFILTERED
ROBERT MONDAVI WINERY

ROBERT MONDAVI WINERY PINOT NOIR RESERVE

...is medium-red in color, with a full, jammy nose, slight hints of raspberry and smoke, beautiful fruit aromas. The taste reflects the nose, jammy and full-flavored. Smooth, long, lingering finish.

SERVE WITH
SAUTÉED DUCK BREASTS WITH OLIVE AND CAPER SAUCE

Sarah Scott, Executive Chef of the Robert Mondavi Wine and Food Center in Costa Mesa, California, created this unique blend of duck, olives and capers to accent this wine of consistently great renown. Although most duck is only obtainable whole, the remainder of the carcasses can either be separately roasted or be used for stock—and duck stock is qualitatively superior when it comes to sauces and gravies; however, some specialty stores do sell only duck breasts. (8 servings)

4 whole Long Island duck breasts, split, deboned, trimmed entirely of fat, which is saved for later use

MARINADE
1 cup Pinot Noir
1 garlic clove, chopped coarsely
1 bay leaf

$1/4$ cup mild olive oil
Fresh ground black pepper

OLIVE CAPER SAUCE
$1/4$ cup Kalamata olives, pitted
$1/4$ cup green olives, pitted (or de-pimientoed)
$1/4$ cup black olives
2 tablespoons olive oil

3 shallots, finely minced
1 garlic clove, finely minced
4 sprigs of thyme, leaves destemmed, chopped fine
$1/4$ cup Pinot Noir
$1/2$-$3/4$ cup chicken stock
1 tablespoon capers, chopped
2 cups rich veal stock

1. Marinate breasts in glass dish with rest of ingredients 1 hour.
2. Combine olives and mince finely, set aside.
3. Heat olive oil in medium sauté pan over medium heat. Add shallots and garlic and cook until soft but not brown.
4. Add olives and chopped thyme, stirring to combine.
5. Add wine and $1/2$ cup chicken stock. Simmer over low heat to reduce for 15-20 minutes.
6. Add the remaining chicken stock and reduce again until mixture is moist but not liquidy. Stir in capers.
7. In separate sauce pan, reduce veal stock by half.
8. Add $1/2$ cup, or more to taste, of olive-caper mixture.
9. Preheat oven to 450°F.
10. Heat sauté pan over medium-high heat. Place some small pieces of the duck fat to render, then remove pieces.
11. Remove breasts from marinade and pat dry. Sprinkle lightly with salt and pepper, and place in hot pan. Sear for about 2 minutes on each side and remove to baking sheet.
12. Cover breasts with the reserved duck fat and place in oven for about 6-8 minutes, depending on the size of the breasts.
13. Remove breasts from the oven, discarding the fat pieces.
14. Slice each breast into 4 pieces, and fan out on each plate. Nap lower half of slices with sauce, and garnish with sprig of fresh thyme.

THE WINE WITH THIS RECIPE
…is grandly improved. Its earthiness and smokiness becomes more apparent, gaining substance behind its hearty fruit flavors. It becomes fuller in the mouth, its body slightly heavier, and its finish is given an extra boost. There is a great Burgundian sense in this wine, and is beautifully paired with this meal.

WESTERN AZALEA

Pinot Noir

SANTA BARBARA COUNTY

PRODUCED AND BOTTLED BY SANFORD WINERY
BUELLTON, CALIFORNIA, U.S.A. ALC. 13.5% BY VOL.

SANFORD PINOT NOIR

…has an enticing garnet color, and expresses sound Burgundian sensibilities of terroir. The wine provides good fruit, brushes across raspberry, some spice, a hint of pepper, of oak, of sweet bell pepper, and is consistently well balanced. It fills the mouth very well, and provides a clean finish.

SERVE WITH
ROASTED VEGETABLES FETTUCCINE

This vegetarian dish from Shirley Sarvis for this wine provides lively food elements that spark with the flavors in a Sanford Pinot Noir. The eggplant becomes almost meaty, bringing a substantial heft, and it actually pushes this dish into the "hearty" category. That, plus the zing the crushed red pepper contributes, and the fresh garden elements from the zucchini and red bell pepper, make this a wonderfully satisfying one-plate meal. (4 servings)

Eggplant, peeled, cut into 1^1/$_2$" by ^{1}/$_2$" by ^{1}/$_2$" strips
  (about 6 cups; 2 medium-sized eggplants)
Salt
Unpeeled zucchini cut in 1^1/$_2$" by ^{1}/$_4$" by ^{1}/$_4$" strips
  (about 4 cups, 1^1/$_3$ lb.)
Red bell pepper (seeds and veins removed), cut into 1^1/$_2$" by ^{1}/$_4$" by
  ^{1}/$_4$" strips (about 1^1/$_3$ cup, 2 large peppers)
10 tablespoons melted unsalted butter
4 teaspoons dry basil, crumbled
^{1}/$_2$ teaspoon ground red pepper flakes
8 ounces dry egg fettuccine, cooked al dente in boiling salted water
  with a little olive oil and well drained
2 tablespoons soft unsalted butter
8-10 tablespoons finely chopped curly parsley

1. Sprinkle eggplant generously with salt; let stand for 20 minutes; wipe dry with paper towels.
2. Turn eggplant, zucchini and red pepper with melted butter, basil and pepper flakes.
3. Spread in a single layer in a shallow baking pan. Bake in a 350°F oven until tender, about 23-25 minutes; stir to turn once or twice.
4. Turn hot pasta with the soft butter and salt to season.
5. Turn pasta with vegetables along with any juices. Lift to warm plates.
6. Sprinkle with parsley.

THE WINE WITH THIS RECIPE

…has its spiciness deliciously raised, the crushed red pepper matching the zip in the wine. It truly releases its fruit, and the bell pepper tones in both wine and meal are cradled together. Scintillating is just the word to describe this experience, as the flavors brightly spark and flash with each other.

STONESTREET PINOT NOIR

...has a red-purple hue, and releases classic barnyard scents, with touches of plum and jam in a most attractive nose. It enjoys depth in the mouth, fruit-laden throughout, big and tannic yet smooth, and the tannins lay down with a smokiness to create an excellent finis to the experience.

SERVE WITH

PAN FRIED JUMBO SEA SCALLOPS WITH SAUTÉED LEEKS, PINOT NOIR SAUCE AND SPICY SUGAR SNAP PEAS

This recipe comes courtesy of Chef Brian Leonard from the winery, and it's a grand combination of flavors and textures to go along with this sumptuous wine. The sauce is a lighter version of a standard shallot wine sauce, and the bright spring taste from the snap peas get an added lift from the spice and the scallops to complete the thought.

PINOT NOIR SAUCE
1 medium shallot, diced
$1^{1}/2$ cups Pinot Noir (Stonestreet)
$1/2$ cup chicken stock or vegetable
   broth
2 tablespoons butter
Salt, to taste

LEEKS AND PEAS
1 large leek
4 tablespoons olive oil
$1/2$ tablespoon chopped ginger
$1/2$ tablespoon chopped garlic
$1/4$ teaspoon crushed red pepper
2 scallions, sliced

1 pound sugar snap peas, washed, strings removed	1$^{1}/_{2}$ pounds jumbo sea scallops
$^{1}/_{4}$ cup water	4 tablespoons flour
	Salt, to taste

FOR THE SAUCE
1. Sauté the shallots until just beginning to clear.
2. Add the wine, reduce until syrup consistency.
3. Add the stock, reduce by $^{1}/_{3}$.
4. On low heat, whisk in the butter, add salt to taste. Keep warm.

FOR THE LEEKS AND PEAS
1. Slice leek in half lengthwise, and slice $^{1}/_{4}$" thick. Rinse thoroughly.
2. Sauté in $^{1}/_{2}$ tablespoon olive oil for 5 minutes on medium heat or until soft and sweet tasting. Set aside.
3. In another pan, heat 1$^{1}/_{2}$ tablespoons oil, and sauté the ginger, garlic, red pepper and scallions for 1$^{1}/_{2}$ minutes.
4. Add the sugar snap peas, sauté for 2 minutes longer.
5. Add the water, cover, and steam for a few minutes.

FOR THE SCALLOPS
1. Lightly dust scallops with flour and salt.
2. Heat olive oil to high heat in a non-stick pan. Sauté the scallops for 1$^{1}/_{2}$ minutes on both sides, or until they become opaque.

TO SERVE
1. Arrange the leeks on a plate in a crescent.
2. Top the leeks with the scallops.
3. Place the sugar snap peas in the center.
4. Drizzle the sauce over the scallops, and serve.

THE WINE WITH THIS RECIPE
…smooths out beautifully, as the spicier elements are elicited from the peas and shallots. The whole character of the wine is enhanced by the process, as the scallops create a creamy, deep accent to its smokiness, and it becomes rounder thanks to the absolutely essential leeks. This is an appealing and ideal match.

ESTATE BOTTLED

TALLEY
VINEYARDS
1993
PINOT NOIR
ARROYO GRANDE VALLEY

TALLEY VINEYARDS PINOT NOIR

...is light-medium purple in color, with sweet cherries and jam in the nose, slightly peppery. Boistrous mouth feel, cherries and jam on full display, with excellent bell pepper characteristics. Typical Central Coast Pinot Noir, excellent fruit, wonderful finish. A glory to behold, and to enjoy.

SERVE WITH
ROASTED RACK OF LAMB WITH PINOT NOIR SAUCE

Jonine Talley kindly provided this recipe to accompany their beautiful Central Coast wine. The marinade seems to take the meat in one direction, then the sauce steers it back, so that the flavors acheive a complexity that matches well with the wine. She suggests you serve this with roasted new potatoes and fresh asparagus. (6 servings)

MARINADE
1 1/2 cups Sauvignon Blanc
    (Talley)
1/4 cup extra virgin olive oil
1 cup coarsely chopped onion
1 tablespoon minced fresh thyme

1 tablespoon minced fresh marjoram
10 cracked black peppercorns
1 bay leaf
LAMB
2 racks of lamb, 9 ribs per rack
Salt, ground pepper, to taste

PINOT NOIR SAUCE
1³/4 cups beef stock (or 1 can [14.5 oz.] beef broth)
1 cup Pinot Noir (Talley)

3 tablespoons unsalted butter
2 shallots, peeled and minced
1 tablespoon flour
Reserved pan juices from the lamb

1. Combine all marinade ingredients in a large bowl and stir well.
2. Trim all visible fat from the lamb racks and discard the fat.
3. Add the lamb to the marinade; cover and let marinate at room temperature for 3-4 hours.
4. Pre-heat the oven to 450°F.
5. Remove the lamb from the marinade, pat dry with paper towels.
6. Set the lamb on a rack in a roasting pan, season well with salt and pepper.
7. Roast the lamb racks for 20-25 minutes, or until an instant reading thermometer registers 130°F for medium rare.
8. Remove from oven, let rest while sauce is being prepared.
9. Combine the beef stock and the red wine in a saucepan. Cook rapidly over high heat until reduced by 1/2.
10. In another saucepan, melt the butter; add the shallots and sauté over low heat for 10 minutes, until the shallots are limp.
11. Add the flour and cook, stirring, for 3 minutes; add the reduced beef stock and whisk over medium heat until the sauce is thickened.
12. Add the pan juices from the lamb racks.
13. Pour the sauce through a fine mesh sieve, pressing hard on the solids to extract all the juices.
14. Keep the sauce warm while finalizing the lamb.
15. Transfer the lamb to a cutting board and slice each lamb rack into individual chops.
16. For each portion, spoon a little of the sauce on a warm dinner plate, and place 3 chops on top of the sauce.

THE WINE WITH THIS RECIPE

…absolutely explodes in the mouth. The tannins become more elegant, as the wine achieves a deeper, fuller structure from the encounter with the flavors in the meal. The cherries/berries enjoy a fresh focus, and the spice in the wine is deliciously promoted by the shallots and herbs in the sauce and marinade.

WILD HORSE™

1994
PINOT NOIR
CENTRAL COAST

PRODUCED AND BOTTLED BY WILD HORSE
TEMPLETON, CALIFORNIA BW 5169 ALC. 12.8 % BY VOL.

WILD HORSE PINOT NOIR

…has a light-medium red color, with a nose that bursts with raspberry, a little hint of cherries and earth, the smells exploding from the glass, a wine draped in elegance. The mouth feel is astounding, it's like taking a bite of fresh fruit, with subtle touches of oak and spice that wrap around the tongue. It leaves a delicious aftertaste. This is a wine that is consistent from first to last sip, a remarkable California Pinot Noir.

Serve with
Warm Mushroom Salad with Raspberry Vinaigrette

Tricia Volk, co-owner with husband Ken of Wild Horse, is an accomplished chef, and has co-written a cookbook with her sister Mary Tartaglione celebrating the wineries of the Central Coast, *Signature Dishes*. Tricia guided this recipe to us for their Pinot Noir. (4 servings)

1 egg yolk
1 tablespoon Dijon mustard
1/3 cup raspberry vinegar
1/2 teaspoon salt
1/4 teaspoon freshly ground
  black pepper
1 cup peanut oil
1 tablespoon unsalted butter
1 shallot, peeled and minced
1/2 lb. mixed fresh mushrooms

(any combination of shiitake, portobello, chanterelle, morel, oyster), cleaned and cut into 1" pieces
6 cups baby organic greens (approx. 1/3 pound)
2 tablespoons minced chives
1/2 cup fresh raspberries, for garnish (optional)

1. In a non-reactive bowl whisk together the egg yolk, mustard, vinegar, salt and pepper.
2. Slowly add the oil, whisking constantly until smooth.
3. Set aside 1/2 cup of the vinaigrette, saving the rest for another use.
4. In a large sauté pan, melt the butter over medium-high heat until the butter begins to brown; add the shallot and mushrooms and cook until the mushrooms begin to soften, about 4 minutes. Season to taste with salt and pepper.
5. Remove pan from heat and add the 1/2 cup vinaigrette.
6. Place the salad greens in a large bowl.
7. Pour the mushroom mixture over the greens and toss quickly.
8. Arrange salad on plates and garnish with chives and raspberries.

The wine with this recipe
…dances with flavors that match and contrast. The raspberry link is stunning, like a key that opens two doors at once: the bitterness of the greens plays with the tannins, the meatiness of the mushrooms links up with the earth tones of the wine, the spiciness comes through. The wine opens up and literally becomes a true friend to the salad. This is one of the finest matches possible.

SYRAH / PETITE SIRAH

*Q*UE SYRAH...SIRAH? Like the Zinfandel, a grape that has flummoxed the wine world as to its true European vinifera origin, there is some confusion as to exactly from what grape varieties both the Syrah and the allegedly non-enologically-related Petite Sirah stem, something that once was described in the 1980s as a sort of "ampelographical tangle." To confound things even more, they seem to exhibit similar flavor components, but never emphatically so. Thankfully, when made well both taste remarkably great—so what ever they are, they are.

It's almost assured the Syrah produced in California is, indeed, the same Syrah grape famous in the Rhone region of France, and there is enough evidence to bear this out, both in how the vines, leaves, and grapes look, and qualitatively how the wines shape up in the bottle. The aroma is typically "smoky," the bouquet scented and floral, and it has a rich, royal purple color; the flavor is hearty, luxuriously dark and lusty, with elements of eucalyptus, smoke, mold, pepper and black currants, a pleasant combination in the mouth to say the least.

The Petite Sirah, on the other hand, has often been guessed to be the Duriff, also from the Rhone region (which might explain some of the original confusion). However, of late it's been suggested that the Petite Sirahs that are sprinkled throughout the state of California could be any one of several Rhone-type varieties, and in some cases may consist of grapes originally chosen from France to be smaller, more intense berries of the Syrah type, hence the "little" or "petite" designation. Nevertheless, as a variety it is capable of producing full-bodied and fruity wines with aromas of black pepper and prunes, that are slow to age.

The wines featured here, taking their cue from their progenitors in the Rhone, are stylistically rich and full-bodied, with a lushness that lends themselvess to the more substantial meal range. With some coaxing, and with a growing list of those who cherish every opportunity to enjoy this varietal, this branch of reds could easily become one of the most popular emerging from the state.

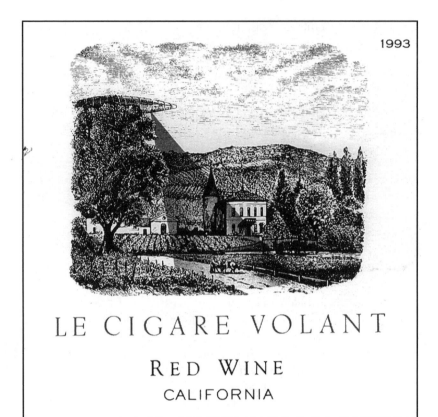

1993

LE CIGARE VOLANT
RED WINE
CALIFORNIA

BONNY DOON LE CIGARE VOLANT

…has a medium red color, with a soft and voluptuous nose, releasing hints of pepper, spice, cherry and a touch of blackberry, quite character-laden. The fruit opens in the mouth, and this Rhone-style wine features its pepperiness and spices well, with a brightness from the tannins accellerating the cherry tones. This is a substantial yet not overbearing wine that tastes great.

SERVE WITH

VEAL CHOPS WITH BLOOD ORANGE, SAGE AND GUAJILLO SAUCE, PURPLE MASHED POTATOES, SWEET CREAMED SPINACH AND GRILLED GREEN ONIONS

This palate- and palette-pleasing recipe comes from the brilliant Chef Hugo Molino at the Parkway Grill in Pasadena, California. If you like your sauce with a little more oomph, double or triple the amount of the otherwise mild guajillo peppers, which are readily available at any Latino grocery store and at most major supermarkets. After looking at the lovely red from the sauce, the lavender hue of the potatoes, the soft green from the spinach, and the sepia tones of the veal, you may think that Chef Hugo was an art director with 20th Century-Fox in another life—definitely Color by Deluxe! He further suggests that you serve this with any vegetable of your choice, if you desire. (4 servings)

BLOOD ORANGE SAGE AND GUAJILLO SAUCE

$1/2$ cup duck stock, semi-reduced
2 ounces shallots, roughly chopped
1 tablespoon fresh garlic
1 dried guajillo pepper, washed, seeded, and soaked in hot water
4 ounces blood orange juice
3 ounces blueberries
4 ounces Marsala
2 ounces butter
2 tablespoons fresh sage, roughly chopped
1 tablespoon honey
Salt, pepper, to taste
1 tablespoon fresh sage, finely chopped

PURPLE MASHED POTATOES

8 ounces purple potatoes (approximately 3 medium-sized)
2 tablespoons unsalted butter
$1/4$ cup half-and-half
Salt, pepper, to taste

SWEET CREAMED SPINACH

1 tablespoon butter
1 teaspoon fresh garlic
2 pounds fresh spinach, washed, no stems
4 ounces heavy cream
2 ounces jack cheese
3 tablespoons sugar
1 ounce parmesan cheese (picorino)
Salt, pepper, to taste

4 veal chops

FOR THE SAUCE

1. Remove guajillo from water, chop it roughly.
2. Sauté garlic and shallots in 1 ounce of butter.
3. Add the chopped guajillo, wine, 2 tablespoons chopped sage, and rest of the other ingredients to the garlic, and cook for about 15 minutes, or until sauce reaches a nice consistency.
4. Strain in fine sieve, and add salt and pepper, to taste.
5. Add remaining tablespoon of finely chopped sage to sauce just prior to serving.

FOR THE POTATOES

1. Pare the potatoes, and chop into quarters.
2. Bring a pot of lightly-salted water to a rolling boil, add the potatoes, and cook for approximately 7 minutes, or until a toothpick can be easily inserted into the potato meat. Drain the water.
3. Place the potatoes in a bowl or food processor equipped with mixers. Add 2 tablespoons of butter and 1/4 cup half-and-half, and whip the potatoes for 2 minutes or until smooth, adding more half-and-half if necessary.

FOR THE SPINACH

1. Sauté garlic in butter until light brown.
2. Add spinach and sauté for about 3 minutes or until spinach completely wilts. Set aside to cool.
3. Place cream, jack cheese and sugar in pot and reduce while stirring constantly until thick. Blend in grated parmesan, and set aside.
4. Drain water from the spinach, then squeeze the spinach to remove as much water as possible, and place in a hot pan.
5. Add cream, and lightly mix together. Season with a pinch of salt and pepper.

TO SERVE

1. Grill the veal chops, along with green onions, to desired doneness.
2. Place cooked chop on plate, drape onions on top, and nap with sauce.
3. Portion out the spinach and mashed potatoes, and serve.

THE WINE WITH THE RECIPE

...*has its flavors accentuated magnificently. The complexities in the wine have a field day with the varieties of flavors in the meal, as it paradoxically becomes smoother yet more forceful. The fruit gains a major sweetness from the blueberries, honey and Marsala, then is twisted by the orange and pepper into a completely new configuration, and with its further pairings (spinach with tannins, potatoes with texture, veal and garlic with fruit), this meal becomes out of this world!*

1993

Notso
PETITE SIRAH
Amador County
ALCOHOL 12.5% BY VOL.

KARLY (NOTSO) PETITE SIRAH

...is deep purple-red in color, with its fruit and spice prominent in the nose, revealing just a trace of fennel. There is full fruit intensity in the mouth, a strong sense of well-balanced spice and pepper, an almost grittiness that bespeaks of style and confidence. With its luscious finish, this is an extremely inviting and desirable wine.

SERVE WITH
KUNG PAO LAMB

This is a fun-to-do involved recipe that came from wine and cooking aficionados Nancy and Bob Klingensmith, who did a masterful job at matching lamb and Petite Sirah with the aggressive glories of this Szechuan hot-pepper favorite. It will involve a trip to your local Asian grocery store to obtain the genuine articles as prescribed here, but with such a delicious wine it should be worth the extra effort. This should be served with steamed white rice. (4 servings)

MARINADE
1 tablespoon soy sauce
1 tablespoon cornstarch
1 tablespoon rice wine (Shao Xing—
    Pagoda brand) or dry sherry
1 lb. leg of lamb, trimmed of fat
    and tendons, cut into 1/2" cubes

SAUCE
1 tablespoon dark soy sauce
    (Pearl River Bridge brand)
1 tablespoon Chinese chili sauce
2 teaspoons unseasoned Japanese
    rice vinegar (Marukan or
    Mitsukan brand)

2 teaspoons sugar
1 teaspoon Japanese sesame oil
1 1/2 teaspoons cornstarch
6 tablespoons chicken stock or water

1/2 cup unsalted raw peanuts (to be roasted)
4 tablespoons peanut or corn oil

4 small, dried red hot chilis, seeded, cut into pieces
2 medium cloves garlic, peeled and sliced on diagonal
4 slices fresh ginger root (U.S. quarter-size coins)
3 scallions (including green tops) cut into 1/4" rounds

1. Combine marinade ingredients in a medium-sized bowl.
2. Add lamb cubes, mix and let marinate at room temperature for 30 minutes.
3. Combine the sauce ingredients in a small bowl and set aside.
4. Pre-heat oven to 350°F.
5. Place peanuts in single layer in shallow pan and roast, stirring frequently, until nuts are lightly golden, about 15 minutes. (Nuts will continue to cook after removal, so do not over-brown them.)
6. Heat wok over high heat.
7. Add 4 tablespoons of peanut oil; swirl it to coat sides of wok.
8. Add chili peppers and stir.
9. Add sliced garlic and ginger and stir to release their aroma.
10. Add the lamb, stir and toss for about 1-2 minutes to sear.
11. Splash 1 tablespoon rice wine on sides of wok, stirring and tossing constantly.
12. Add the cut-up scallions and continue to stir-fry in the same manner for 30-45 seconds.
13. Stir the sauce ingredients and add mixture to the wok, continuing to toss and stir while sauce thickens.
14. Add the roasted peanuts, stir to mix, and serve.

THE WINE WITH THIS RECIPE

...has its spiciness cleverly enveloped by the food and spices. The experience is not the harsh fire-in-mouth quality often associated with Kung Pao, but with the robust lamb and the balanced wine the meal becomes disconcertingly attractive, almost addictive. This is truly a wonderful pairing that will continue to surprise as you adapt new ways to combine this wine with this style of cooking.

THE OJAI VINEYARD SYRAH

…is rich purple/deep garnet in color, with outstanding spiciness in the nose, along with red cherries, all indicating excellent balance. It provides a medium feel in the mouth, its enticing spice grabbing you right away without being heavy handed. A fine Rhone wine, well-balanced, full in character, and providing a most satisfying finish.

SERVE WITH
SPICY BONELESS PORK LOIN ROAST

Adam and Helen Tolmach, owners of the winery, took time from their busy schedules to help provide this recipe. Adam is a free-wheeling cook who rarely measures ingredients as he goes, so there is room for expanding or contracting amounts, but based on our tests these are just about perfect. (4 servings)

2 tablespoons California chile powder (or other medium-hot chile powder)*
2 tablespoons ground cumin
2 tablespoons ground coriander
1/2 teaspoon salt
1/2 teaspoon black pepper
2-3 lb. boneless pork tenderloin
5 medium cloves garlic
Fresh rosemary branches (or dried rosemary leaves)

1. Combine the dry ingredients together in a small bowl.
2. Open the two halves of the loins or, if a single roll, butterfly it.
3. Press the garlic cloves into slits cut into the opened roast "interior" and then sprinkle a generous amount of the spice mixture there as well.
4. Fold it back, then tie up the roast using cotton string (your butcher should give you some if you ask).
5. Roll the roast in the rest of the spice mixture until it is completely coated.
6. Using a domed kettle cooker, place the rosemary branches on the grill as a "bed" for the meat, to inhibit burning.
7. Barbecue the pork on medium-heat coals with the lid on, vented for smoke.
8. Turn once during cooking, at which time insert a thermometer.
9. Cook to an internal temperature of 155°F for pink and juicy, 175°F for well done.
(The roast can also be cooked in a glass pan in the oven. Forego the bed of rosemary, but do sprinkle the roast with dried rosemary leaves and cook at 350°F.)

* Please refer to fresh chile powder recipe in Appendix C.

THE WINE WITH THIS RECIPE
…has its spices almost integrated with the food. The body weight of the wine is exactly what the pork meat calls for. The flavors of the wine and the meal coordinate throughout, neither intruding on the other but both clearly complementing each other. More fruit in the wine is revealed, it becomes intensified as it opens to the encounter. The Tolmachs know their wine and their cooking!

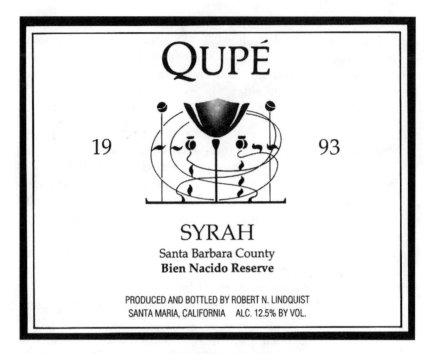

QUPÉ SYRAH
BIEN NACIDO RESERVE

...looks delicious in the glass, deep dark rich purple, then presents a nose with wondrous spice and fruit, complex, earthy, bold, a standard-bearer. It laces the tongue with degrees of boysenberry and blackberry, pepper, wildly drinkable. The flavors reverberate throughout the finish, and emphatically certifies this as a substantial, supreme California Syrah.

SERVE WITH
GRILLED LAMB CHOPS WITH SAUTÉED ROOT VEGETABLES

This classy rendition of a barbecue favorite comes from Donna Oken, who is involved in the major Central Coast winemaking coalition that has made that area's product so remarkable: Bob Lindquist of Qupé working with Jim Clendenon of Au Bon Climat and/or Ken Volk of Wild Horse, and others, to share minds, blends and business. To complete the meal she's fashioned around this wine, she recommends a light salad of baby spinach with balsamic vinaigrette that should include blue cheese crumbles and chopped toasted pecans.

Lamb Chops, 1 per person, thick-cut
1/4 cup extra virgin olive oil
1 tablespoon each fresh oregano, thyme, sage, rosemary
    and garlic, chopped
2 each carrots and parsnips
1 rutabaga
2-4 tablespoons butter
1/8 teaspoon nutmeg
Salt, pepper

1. Marinate the lamb chops in a mixture of the oil, herbs and garlic inside a resealable plastic bag in the refrigerator overnight.
2. Peel and slice the carrots and parsnips on the diagonal; peel the rutabaga, slice in half, and then in thin slices.
3. Steam the vegetables for 15 minutes.
4. Heat the butter in a pan, and sauté the steamed vegetables with salt, pepper and nutmeg for about 10 minutes, or until golden.
5. Grill the lamb over medium-high heat for 5 minutes on each side for medium-rare, or until desired doneness.
6. Serve lamb with vegetables, along with recommended salad.

THE WINE WITH THE RECIPE

…has its pepper and spice accentuated, and its fruit becomes opulent and lusty. The herbs gracing the lamb blend with the spice in the wine, and the surprising contribution from the root vegetables lends a creaminess, earthiness, and sweetness to the mix, especially the underappreciated rutabaga, and may provide the unexperienced fresh pleasures from food. The wine clearly enjoys its relationship with this recipe, making it more fruit-bearing and hearty, an extremely satisfying match.

STAG'S LEAP WINE CELLARS PETITE SIRAH

…is medium-deep red ruby in color, with a hefty dose of jammy and berry fruit in the nose, along with a nice spark of spice. It is very intense in the mouth, lots of pepper and full, rich taste, a little gamey, almost chewy. With its finish cradling the tongue, this is an excellent wine experience.

SERVE WITH
**SAVORY GOAT CHEESE AND
ROASTED RED PEPPER TART WITH ROSEMARY**

This is a unique, substantive, large-flavored dish as developed at the winery. As such, its hugeness is not for the faint of heart—but the reward is up to the challenge! The myriad flavors involved in its creation mirror the complexity of the wine, and is worth composing. (8 servings)

CRUST

2 cups all-purpose flour

1/4 teaspoon salt

6 ounces unsalted butter

2 1/2 -3 ounces water

TART FILLING

2 leeks, cut into 2" lengths, julienned and washed

1 red bell pepper, oiled

1 head garlic, peeled, then "chunked"

3 ounces Laura Chenel goat cheese (or a fine chevret goat cheese)

1/2 cup olive oil

2 eggs

2 egg yolks

1 1/2 cups half-and-half

1/2 teaspoon salt

1/2 teaspoon crushed white pepper

1/4 teaspoon cayenne

1 tablespoon fresh rosemary leaves

FOR THE CRUST

1. In a large bowl combine the flour and salt.

2. Cut the butter into small pieces and add it to the flour. Blend the butter into the flour with your hand working quickly so as not to warm the butter. Mix until the flour is fairly evenly mixed and the mixture is of a coarse, granular consistency.

3. Refrigerate the flour mixture and, in a separate cup, the water.

4. Remove both after 10 minutes and add three quarters of the water to the flour and butter. Mix until a loose, crumbly ball can be formed. (Add all of the water if necessary.)

5. Put the dough in a plastic bag and put it in the refrigerator to rest for one hour.

6. When thoroughly chilled, roll the dough out and place it in a 12" tart shell.

7. Cover shell with a sheet of aluminum foil and fill it with dry beans.

8. Bake shell in a 425°F oven for 7-9 minutes.

9. Remove the beans and foil from the shell, prick the shell with a fork and return it to the oven for another 4 minutes, or until it begins to brown.

FOR THE TART

1. Preheat oven to 275°F.
2. Place the garlic in an oven-safe pan and add the olive oil. Place on medium heat and bring up to a simmer.
3. Place the pan in the oven and bake for 15 minutes, or until the cloves are light golden brown.
4. Increase the oven temperature to 400°F.
5. Oven roast the oiled red pepper, turning occasionally, until the skin is loose and the pepper is slightly brown, about 40 minutes.
6. When done, turn off oven, remove pepper and place it in a covered bowl in the refrigerator. After the pepper is cool, remove the skin, stem, seeds, and membrane walls, reserving the liquid that the pepper gives off.
7. Cut the pepper into 2" julienne strips, and reserve.
8. Using one tablespoon of oil from the roasted garlic, sweat the julienned leeks until they are soft and just begininng to brown.
9. Add the julienned peppers and liquid to the leeks. Reduce heat and allow the liquid to evaporate.
10. Pre-heat oven to 350°F.
11. In a medium bowl, beat the eggs and egg yolks together.
12. Add the half-and-half, salt, pepper, and cayenne, and mix thoroughly.
13. Place the leeks and peppers in the tart shell, leaving the center of the shell open, to make the tart easier to cut.
14. Drain off the oil from the garlic cloves and place the whole cloves in the tart shell.
15. Add small pieces of goat cheese around the tart.
16. Pour enough of the egg mixture into the shell to fill it 3/4 full.
17. Sprinkle the rosemary over the tart.
18. Bake 25-35 minutes or until lightly browned on top. Remove and serve warm with the wine.

THE WINE WITH THIS RECIPE

...has its pleasantness increased lovingly. With the cheese, peppers and leeks, along with the heady garlic, confronting the spiciness in the fruit, both come away improved by the encounter. The flavors, including the flash of gaminess in the wine, mesh well, and create a full-bodied engagement.

ZINFANDEL

*I*F THERE'S ONE WINE GRAPE variety that can be truly called mysterious, it is the Zinfandel. Virtually all other varietals can be traced back to a specific location or area, often well-documented over the centuries. Not so the Zinfandel. This remarkable grape found its way to California in the 19th Century, mislabeled or unlabeled, acquired the name "Zinfandel" (perhaps from the Hungarian-based Zinfardel, which it in no way resembles), then immediately established itself as a primary source for California red wine.

The grape has produced much speculation as to its origins. In 1977, Dr. Austin Goheen of UC-Davis declared it to be an Italian grape, the Primitivo di Gioia. However, Dr. Charles L. Sullivan at the same institution published in 1982 that it's the Black St. Peters. These are only the two most noteworthy guesses among several others, but the nod now seems to go to the Primitivo, thanks to some recent ampelographical DNA testing that has been quite conclusive.

Now, how it got here is equally

mysterious. Although once believed to have been brought to California by the redoubtable entrepreneur and wine industry pioneer Agoston Haraszthy (who among other things was San Diego's first sheriff and was ultimately eaten by alligators in the Amazon), it's now clear this claim was the fabrication of his son Arpad, long after the fact, in an attempt to make his bombastic father seem even more legendary. From these shadowy beginnings the Zinfandel emerged from the pack of countless varieties being test planted throughout the state, having satisfied growers and consumers alike, and has been going strong for well over a century.

Fine Zinfandels are frequently noted for their deep purple color and intense "bramble" qualities: blackberry, raspberry, boysenberry flavors, lush and fruity. Red-sauced pasta is an automatic pairing, but so are rich cheeses like Stilton, Gloucestershire, Camembert, along with all fruits. Although originally consumed "young" and not regarded as a lay-down varietal, many wineries are finding that several years of bottle age with their more elegant Zinfandels are producing subtleties they hadn't anticipated with earlier releases. The wines that follow are remarkable examples of how transcendent such Zinfandels can be, and how well they can be accompanied by a diverse range of taste pairings.

CAYMUS VINEYARDS ZINFANDEL

…features a deep, rich red color, and has a full, rich nose, lots of fruit, hints of spice, of pepper, of eucalyptus, a little tobacco. There is a small explosion of flavor in the mouth with the flavors all emerging, underneath a good tannin structure.

SERVE WITH
CASSOULET OF LENTILS VERTES DU PUY WITH LAMB, SAUSAGE AND PORK

A simple legume stew with link sausage from any kind of game, but if hard pressed a highly-seasoned substitute can do nicely. The small-ish lentils act as bland flavor receptors that marry well with the other ingredients. Thus, it's best to cook this at least a day (or more) in advance in order to meld the flavors. This recipe originally came from Napa Valley's Brava Terrace Restaurant by owner Fred Halpert, and the winery passed it on for home adaptation. (8 servings)

1 carrot, diced
1 medium onion, diced
2 celery stalks, diced
1/4 cup olive oil
1 pound lentils from Puy
1 bay leaf

2 sprigs of thyme
2+ cups chicken stock
1 pound pork loin
1/2 tablespoon ground cumin
1 pound specialty link sausage
 (duck, venison)

1 pound leg of lamb, trimmed
1 garlic clove, peeled and slivered
1 pound mushrooms, quartered
Salt

White pepper
2 tablespoons unsalted butter
1 bunch chives, chopped

1. Sauté carrot, onion and celery in olive oil over medium heat until onions begin to become translucent.
2. Add lentils, bay leaf and thyme, and sauté approximately 1 minute.
3. Add enough chicken stock to completely cover lentils, bring to boil, then cover and cook for 25+ minutes on medium heat until lentils just begin to pass the al dente stage, stirring occasionally— then remove from heat and set aside.
4. Pre-cook the sausages in a 400°F oven for 15 minutes.
5. Cut the pork loin in half, season with a dusting of cumin, salt and pepper.
6. Cut the lamb in half, and cram the slivers of garlic into slits cut into the meat; add salt and pepper.
7. Sear the meats until rare—do not overcook pork (it dries out), nor undercook lamb (raw is not rare)—then remove lamb and pork from pan.
8. Remove sausages from oven, sear them in same pan.
9. When cool enough not to bring welts to your fingers, cut all the meat into bite-sized portions.
10. Sauté quartered mushrooms separately in butter.
11. Return lentils to heat, and add all ingredients to lentils and cook until meats reach desired degree of doneness, then season to taste.
12. Place entire meal into the refrigerator for at least 24 hours.
13. When ready to serve, reheat the cassoulet, then ladle into individual serving bowls, being sure to include some of all three meats, and add chopped chives for garnish.

THE WINE WITH THIS RECIPE

...expands wonderfully, as all its flavor attributes are given free rein to interact with the substantial elements in the stew. The wine becomes more refined, its smoothness defined, as its fruit becomes more potent, the heady characteristics of Zinfandel beautifully exposed. This is definitely a food wine, and this is the right kind of food to make it work.

GRGICH HILLS

Sonoma County
ZINFANDEL
1992

CELLARED AND BOTTLED BY GRGICH HILLS CELLAR
RUTHERFORD, CA · ALC. 13.7% BY VOL. · CONTAINS SULFITES

GRGICH HILLS ZINFANDEL

…is medium-red in color, and reveals tons of cherry and berry fruit in the nose, along with a thread of oak and spice, lots of depth. Once in the mouth, it only gets better: full, rich, good oak, excellent tannin structure, it erupts with flavor, spice, fruit, with a finish that refuses to dissipate. This is big-time Zinfandel, what a delicious wine should taste like.

SERVE WITH
CHICKEN WITH PINE NUTS

Chef Angelo Auriano of the famed Los Angeles restaurant Valentino provided this white meat/red wine crossover. Appropriately, there are some exciting taste combinations meant to interact with this heady, flavorful wine. The brown sauce, itself a major flavoring agent, acts as a link with the "meat" side of the palate with the otherwise easy flavoring in the poultry. A zingy, bright and boistrous meal. (8 servings)

8 boneless, skinless chicken breasts
1/2 cup flour (or as needed)
1/2 cup cooking oil
1/3 cup butter
1 1/4 cups pine nuts
4 cloves garlic, minced

1 cup dry white wine
2 lemons, juiced
1 bunch parsley, chopped
2 cups Brown Sauce, heated
1/2 teaspoon salt (or to taste)
1/4 teaspoon pepper (or to taste)

1. Pre-heat oven to 350°F.
2. Thoroughly coat the chicken breasts with the flour.
3. In a large skillet, heat the oil on medium-high until hot. Add chicken breasts and sauté them 3-4 minutes on each side, or until golden brown.
4. Remove the chicken breasts and place them in a large baking dish. Cover the dish and keep the chicken warm.
5. Drain the oil out of the skillet. Add butter and heat on medium-high until melted.
6. Add the pine nuts and sauté for 1-2 minutes, or until golden brown.
7. Spread the pine nuts on baking sheet, and briefly roast to lightly crisp.
8. Return the pine nuts to the sauté pan. Add the garlic and wine, and cook together for 3-4 minutes, or until the wine has evaporated.
9. Add lemon juice, parsley, heated brown sauce, salt and pepper. Stir the ingredients together.
10. Pour the sauce over the chicken.
11. Bake the chicken for 15 minutes or until thoroughly hot.

THE WINE WITH THIS RECIPE
...becomes even smoother, with its spiciness being accented roundly. The pine nuts give a lot of flavor, and for a match between chicken and Zinfandel it makes a statement, with the tannin structure holding up well.

1993

NALLE

SONOMA COUNTY
DRY CREEK VALLEY

ZINFANDEL

ALC. 13.5% BY VOL.

PRODUCED AND BOTTLED BY NALLE WINERY
HEALDSBURG, CALIFORNIA

NALLE WINERY ZINFANDEL

...is medium-red in color, with an attractive, classic nose, lots of fruit, spice, and berry to the max. The mouth-feel is luxurious, as the flavors burst alive, blackberry, lingonberry, boysenberry—what Doug Nalle refers to as "Zinberry!" Balanced perfectly, full and medium-rich in flavor, with a finish that lingers, this is consistently one of the fine wines in California.

SERVE WITH

VENISON STEAKS WITH ZINFANDEL,
CHIPOTLE ROASTED SHALLOTS AND PECAN SAUCE

Doug Nalle kindly orchestrated this suggestion via Mixx Restaurant in Santa Rosa, California, as created by its owners, Dan and Kathleen Berman. It tastes as interesting as it sounds, and given the personal nature of Nalle Winery, this is a special meal indeed. Although canned chipotles are available, they're often in a tomato-based sauce which is not in keeping with this recipe—so wash it off. (2 servings)

Two 5 ounce venison steaks, center cut (1^{1}/2 " thick)
Kosher salt & cracked black peppercorns
Oil (for searing steaks)
VENISON SAUCE
^{1}/2 chipotle en escabeche, seeds removed and julienned
6 shallots, peeled and roasted
^{1}/4 cup Zinfandel (Nalle)
1 tablespoon molasses
^{1}/2 cup demi glace (see Appendix B)
1 tablespoon butter, softened

Salt & pepper
6 toasted pecan halves per person

1. Lightly season venison steaks with Kosher salt and pepper.
2. Set a skillet over high heat and film pan with oil. When oil begins to smoke, add the steaks and sear 2-3 minutes on one side, until brown and crusty; turn steaks over and sear for another 2 minutes.
3. Remove from pan—meat should feel rare, not quite firm; set aside and keep warm.
4. Pour excess oil from pan. Add chipotle and shallots and heat quickly without burning.
5. Add wine, reduce by half.
6. Add molasses and demi-glace. Reduce until sauce is rich-looking and shiny, or evenly coats the back of a spoon.
7. Whisk in butter. Season carefully with salt and pepper (taking into account the spice of chipotle).
8. Place steaks on a platter, spoon sauce over them, place 6 pecans on top, and serve immediately.

THE WINE WITH THIS RECIPE
…has its components heightened, expanded and blessed. The fruit increases in complexity and smoothness, as the spices in the sauce elevate the spices in the wine almost mystically. It's dangerous to use the word perfect, but this is.

RIDGE 1993 CALIFORNIA LYTTON SPRINGS®

RIDGE ZINFANDEL
LYTTON SPRINGS

...enjoys a deep dark ruby color, and sports a truly great Zinfandel nose, with tangents of pepper, spice, blackberry, very full and rich. In the mouth there's totality, great tannin structure. The fruit becomes even more glorious, a solid body, and it flows like liquid marmalade in the finish. Complex and tremendous.

SERVE WITH

GAME WITH MEXICAN COCOA, ZINFANDEL AND BLACK CHILE SAUCE

This recipe was created by Hugo Molina of Pasadena's famed Parkway Grill Restaurant. Although he originally called for antelope, Chef Hugo allows that this recipe can also be used with other meats as well, including veal and poultry. If you are fortunate to obtain some antelope, be careful not to overcook it, because it can turn quite tough—and, unfortunately, the meat is so dark it's hard to tell! The spices are most unusual: you'll need to render a pasilla chile into the powder state, and the Mexican cocoa usually comes in solid cake form but melts easily. (4 servings)

8 ounces Zinfandel (Ridge)
3 ounces shallots, chopped medium
1 teaspoon fresh garlic, chopped
3 ounces unsalted butter
1 1/2 ounces Mexican cocoa

1 ounce black chile powder
(see Appendix C)
8 ounces reduced duck or veal stock
1 ounce balsamic vinegar
2 1/2 pounds tenderloins of game
(or veal or poultry)

TO MAKE SAUCE

1. Sauté shallots and garlic in 1 ounce butter until light brown.
2. Add wine, cocoa, chile powder and stock. Cook for about 3 minutes or reduce until mixture coats the back of a spoon nicely. Remove from the heat.
3. Add a pinch of salt and pepper and the vinegar.
4. Incorporate the remaining butter and strain.

TO COOK & SERVE MEAT

1. Cook on grill or bake to desired doneness.
2. Cut meat in medallions and place on plates with desired vegatables.
3. Pour sauce over meat and serve hot.

THE WINE WITH THIS RECIPE

...blends beautifully with the food, with the spice in both in complete harmony. The food brings out the sumptuous dark qualities in the wine, as the mild gaminess in the meat toys with the fruit and creates a thrilling taste mood. The chocolate-chile sauce provides the finish with a deepening that carries out its themes to an incredible end. This is awesome.

STORYBOOK MOUNTAIN VINEYARDS ZINFANDEL

...is deep, dark red in the glass, and offers a full, peppery nose, full of boy-senberry characteristics, a very appealing, luscious nose with lots of fruit elements. It is full and peppery-tasting in the mouth, well-rounded and fruity, with an excellent finish, sweetness in the fruit of the aftertaste with a small burst of acid remaining. A fine and finely complex wine.

SERVE WITH
LE CHAPEAU DU COCHON STORYBOOK

Truly a pastry "hat" that is baked with meat, vegetables and cheese inside, this one course meal from the kitchen of the winery is fun to make, to present, and to eat, plus you make it in advance to bake at your convenience. (4 servings)

PASTRY	FILLING
3/4 cup white flour	1 pound marbled pork, in small
1/2 cup whole wheat flour	chunks (steaks, roast or chops
1/4 pound butter	with fat and gristle removed)
1/2 cup small curd cottage cheese	1 tablespoon olive oil

1 pinch nutmeg
Ground pepper to taste
6 green onions, tops included,
   sliced fine
2-3 celery stalks, chopped fine

1 egg
2 tablespoons water
2/3 pound cheese, shredded
   (Gruyere, kasseri or asiago)

To make pastry
1. Blend the flours and butter in food processor.
2. Blend in cottage cheese until ball forms.
3. Form into a fat disk, wrap in cellophane, refrigerate.

To make filling
1. Sauté pork in olive oil until browned.
2. Add nutmeg, pepper and green onions and cook 2 minutes longer.
3. Add celery and cook until soft.
4. Remove mixture, allow to cool.

Final preparation
1. Remove dough from refrigerator, cut dough in half down middle to create two disks.
2. Roll out half the dough into a large round and place on lightly oiled baking sheet. Put half the cheese on top. Add filling, then remaining cheese.
3. Mix egg together with water; brush edge of pastry with it (to serve as "glue").
4. Roll out rest of dough into matching, slightly larger version of original shape, cover mixture and crimp the edge together to create "brim" of hat.
5. Brush top with egg and water mixture.
6. Allow to rest 2-12 hours in refrigerator.
7. Bake in preheated 400°F oven for approximately 25 minutes. Pastry will be a flecked golden brown.
8. Cool for 5 minutes on a rack, then serve.

The wine with this recipe
...enjoys a fresh perspective on what Zinfandels go with. Even though the pork is light, it holds up well to the wine, its pepper actually making the pork more flavorful and vice versa. Along with the green onion's flavors kicking in, the nuttiness from the cheese brings out interesting facets in the wine.

CABERNET SAUVIGNON

*T*HERE IS A GENUINE SENSE of awe when one encounters a Cabernet Sauvignon of elegance, grace and stature. Here is a wine steeped in history, both political and vinicultural, a wine that for centuries defined what French red wine was for the rest of the world, and how much progress has been made in California.

The Cabernet Sauvignon grape made its first appearance as a "varietal" when Monsieur Arnaud de Pontac issued the first estate wine from Bordeaux in 1660, Château Haut-Brion, and it became the wine of choice in London by the second half of the 17th century. (It was, of course, primarily Cabernet Sauvignon, as it is today.) How much of this wine was actually Cabernet Sauvignon cannot be determined, as the wineries of that day were more concerned with establishing a selective estate designation, and this "claret" so preferred by the British most certainly involved an aggregation of whatever grapes had been serendipitously planted generations earlier. However, after the French Revolution, M. Lamonthe, a manager of the Château Latour estate, proceeded to remove what he determined were less desirable vines, and replant or graft them to the Cabernet Sauvignon variety almost exclusively. His efforts were then widely imitated throughout that region, which is why to this day "Bordeaux" and "Cabernet Sauvignon" are almost synonymous.

Cabernet Sauvignon arrived in California around the 1880s, among a slew of other wines that were being planted with experimental abandon throughout the state. At that time, varietal quality was less an issue than was production volume, the overwhelming desire for merely a drinkable "claret" the guiding factor. Nevertheless, even then, Cabernet Sauvignon was the predominant red grape being grown in the state. After the repeal of prohibition, California began to significantly concentrate on specific varietals as a means of differentiating itself from France—with Cabernet Sauvignon leading the bandwagon.

Although California Cabernet Sauvignon had a span of big, overbearing releases during the late 1960s and through the 1970s, some wineries maintained their focus on more elegant and balanced Bordeaux-style vintages. When the Stag's Leap Wine Cellars 1973 Cabernet Sauvignon was entered in the 1976 Bicentennial Tasting competition in Paris, it was deemed as fine a wine as any in the world; this resoundingly shook up the world's perception of France as being the world's single provider of the world's finest Cabernet Sauvignon-based wines, which the French had cultivated for centuries. (As for white wines, an identical feat was accomplished at the same competition by Napa's Chateau Montelena, its 1973 Chardonnay besting the best French white Burgundies.) California wine, and Napa in particular, reaped enormous benefits.

As to the grape itself, Cabernet Sauvignon grows heartily but capriciously. The buds open late (thus avoiding spring frosts such as occur in Napa); the bunches are small and irregularly shaped, but the berries are black, perfect globes, packed tightly. The resulting wine can carry such flavors as violets, lavender, black currants, eucalyptus, tar, chocolate, charcoal—all, in this context, desirable and pleasant.

After fermentation, Cabernet Sauvignon is almost uniformly aged in oak. Although some wineries use American oak, most rely on French oak, new and used. Tannin levels can vary from vineyard to vineyard, and the intensities depend on the vines and each winemaker's choice. Optimally, a well-structured, delicious Cabernet Sauvignon in its youth can transform itself through the bottle-aging process into a wine of depth, complexity of flavor and luxurious definition, something well worth the wait for the patient.

Most Cabernet Sauvignons are blended with other wines, two in particular, Merlot and Cabernet Franc. Both are used to soften, with the Merlot also adding fruit, the Cabernet Franc a bit of fragrance. In fact, since the mid-1980s Merlot has carved a market niche for itself as its own variety, being pliant and more berry-like in flavor, extremely pleasing qualities. Thanks to champions such as Dan Duckhorn, it has risen to peer status, and is so included here as an equal member of the royal Bordeaux family.

Once any variety in a bottle of wine drops below the 75% minimum required by U.S. law to maintain varietal status, it then must be called something else. For Bordeaux-type wines, including whites, the term "meritage" is often applied by some wineries to identify them as such. Also, some wineries deliberately choose not to use any varietal name with their Bordeaux, even though they exceed the 75% minimum to a large degree, in order to create a "Chateau"-type identity of their own.

Whether one can wait the (in some cases long) years for a responsive Cabernet Sauvignon to reach its peak is a personal matter. Thankfully, there are many fine wine shops that keep aged Cabernet Sauvignon on hand from vintages past for your enjoyment. Let it simply be said that, when it comes to expressions of excellence in wine, there may be no finer or memorable example than a superb Cabernet Sauvignon.

Cakebread Cellars

NAPA VALLEY

Cabernet Sauvignon

1990

CAKEBREAD CELLARS CABERNET SAUVIGNON
...features a deep, dark red color, and exhibits typical Napa Valley floor nose, with hints of oak, eucalyptus, a touch of tobacco, and provides a pleasing berry character. In the mouth, its fruit emerges, revealing excellent balance, the tannins just right, with a fine finish. All in all, a fruity, berry-ish, lively wine.

SERVE WITH
VENISON STEW WITH DRIED CHERRIES

A meal that almost hearkens back to Pilgrim days, a hearty, robust dish perfect for cold winter nights, cool fall nights, brisk spring nights, or even tepid summer nights. This is a stellar creation of Dolores Cakebread and the winery's resident chef Brian Streeter. (8 servings)

2 1/2 pounds boneless venison stew meat, well trimmed
Flour (as needed)
Pepper, to taste
Olive oil (as needed)
2 cups onion, diced large
2 cups carrots, diced
1 cup celery, diced
1/2 orange

8-10 juniper berries, cracked
6-8 garlic cloves
3 ounces tomato paste
2 cups red wine (Cakebread)
2 cups venison or beef stock
8 medium red potatoes
1/4 cup dried cherries
1/4 cup Brandy
Fuselli or other small-sized pasta

1. Cut venison into 1" cubes. Roll in peppered flour, brown in hot oil in large pan, remove.
2. Add onions, carrots and celery to the pan; sauté until onions are lightly caramelized. Add orange, juniper berries, and garlic. Sauté until garlic releases its aroma. Add tomato paste and sauté until lightly caramelized.
3. Add red wine, gently scraping pan to release any residue; reduce sauce by half.
4. Add stock, bring to a boil. Return venison to pan, adding extra stock if necessary to just barely cover the meat. Return to a boil, then reduce heat, cover, and simmer for 1 1/2 hours, stirring on occasion. (Can be put in 350°F over for 1 1/2 hours, covered, stirring every half hour.)
5. Add potatoes and cherries, cook (bake) another hour or until meat is tender.
6. Add Brandy during last half hour. (Add more wine or water if more liquid is needed.) Adjust seasoning.
7. Serve on a bed of cooked pasta—we recommend fuselli, as the coils pick up the stew fluid well.

THE WINE WITH THIS RECIPE
...is gorgeously cranked up several notches from its already glorious level. The earthiness of both wine and food are woven so tightly together they seem destined to be paired. The orange tweaks the berry in the wine here, then the cherries tweak the dark cherry in the wine there, and the venison locks horns with the tannins in a stunning display of most agreeable forces. The compelling end result is one of the most perfect wine-food matches there is.

CARMENET MERITAGE
MOON MOUNTAIN

...is dark ruby red, and features a deep cherry nose, a hint of tea leaves, and aromas of oak, clover and eucalyptus. It swings rich and full in the mouth, revealing excellent tannin structure, with quality spice and fruit in full evidence. The smooth, clean finish via the Merlot finesse creates a complete taste package with classy intensity. This is mountain fruit at its best.

SERVE WITH
BRAISED BEEF SHORT RIBS

This part barbecue-part oven bake comes from Michael Chiarello of Napa Valley's Tra Vigne Restaurant. The meat is marinated in an herbed brown sugar-brine solution, then seared on a barbecue, and placed in reduced broth with vegetables and baked until done. Served with the reduced braising liquid as sauce, this is a flavorful process that calmly provides a hearty main course. (4-6 servings)

1 gallon Basic Brown Sugar Brine	1 large carrot, rough chop
1 gallon water	3 celery ribs, rough chop
2 cups brown sugar	1 garlic head, cut in half sideways
2 cups kosher or sea salt	1 cup beef stock
2 bay leaves	1/2 cup red wine (Carmenet)
10 juniper berries	1/4 cup sherry vinegar
4-8 2" beef short ribs	1/4 cup crushed tomatoes
2 tablespoons extra virgin olive oil	1 tablespoon fresh chopped oregano
2 medium onions, rough cut	Oregano sprigs, for garnish

FOR THE MARINADE

Combine the brine ingredients in a heavy gauge pot, bring to a boil, then let cool. Place the meat in the brine for one hour (can be done up to 2 days in advance). Remove meat from the brine and pat dry.

TO PREPARE MEAT

1. On a barbecue grill over medium heat, sear the meat to a golden brown (can be done up to a day [or night] ahead).
2. In a braising pan, caramelize the vegetables in the olive oil on high heat. Add the wine, reducing until almost dry, then add the beef stock and vinegar. Place the ribs into this liquid, bring to a simmer, cover and place in a pre-heated 300°F oven for three hours, or until tender. Remove the ribs from the pan, set aside and keep warm.
3. Strain the braising liquid into a medium sauce pan; add the crushed tomato and reduce over medium-high heat until the sauce coats the back of a wooden spoon. Stir in the chopped oregano.

TO SERVE

Place the ribs on individual plates, nap with the sauce, garnish with fresh sprigs of oregano, and serve.

THE WINE WITH THIS RECIPE

…has its fruit intensity exposed. The smoothness is remarkable in concert with the meat's seasonings. A note of spiciness emerges from the wine, and new complexities of flavor are created by the tomato and oregano sauce against the fruit in the wine.

CAYMUS VINEYARDS CABERNET SAUVIGNON

...is *beautifully rich red in color, with a nose that yields tobacco, pepper, cassis, berry, and oak, simply gorgeous fruit notes. All this expands once in the mouth, lots of berry, attractive spice and pepper, the oak waiting until the last moment to present itself. A smooth, persistent finish, this is a superbly-structured wine.*

Serve with
RCK Raspberry Barbecued Lamb

Ron Breitstein, along with culinary adventuring friends Chris Beck and Kelly Gill, created this wine-specific inspired meal. Rothschild's Raspberry Barbecue sauce is available in selected gourmet stores, or you can make your own version by using any top-grade sauce, add a healthy dose of raspberry vinegar and some brown sugar and molasses, and taste to adjust. (4-9 servings)

2 tablespoons fresh rosemary, finely chopped
1-2 cups Rothschild's Raspberry BBQ sauce
2-5 pound leg of lamb—butterflied

1. Mix the rosemary into the barbecue sauce.
2. Open leg of lamb, slather the exposed interior surface of the lamb with raspberry-rosemary sauce, then fold it back over. Bind the lamb with three loops of butcher's twine.
3. Coat the lamb with the sauce, then begin cooking on a barbecue grill with closed lid, being careful to keep the coated meat at enough distance from the coals not to burn.
4. After at least 20 minutes, turn the lamb over. Recoat the cooked "up" side with more sauce, and continue cooking for another 20-25 minutes, or until desired doneness.
5. Turn over again, slather more sauce, and close lid for an additional 5 minutes.
6. Slice thin, and serve with sautéed zucchini and yellow squash, or with artichokes.

The wine with this recipe
…has its fullness and smoothness really come out, its spice teaming well with the rosemary, its berry-fruit meshing with the raspberry. With the deep flavor of the lamb enjoying the dark tones of the wine, this proves to be an excellent match.

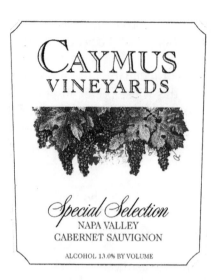

CAYMUS VINEYARDS CABERNET SAUVIGNON
SPECIAL SELECTION

…has a lustrously deep ruby color, with lush fruit in the nose, lots of jammy berry, with latent wood tones and tobacco—it expands even further after some minutes in the glass. It provides a satisfying fullness in the mouth, with the berry allowed to keep its presence thanks to a gentle tannin structure, as the finish trails off ethereally.

SERVE WITH
GRILLED FILET OF BEEF
WITH PARSNIP MASHED POTATOES

As created by Fred Halpert at Brava Terrace Restaurant in Napa's St. Helena specifically for this wine, this is a basic, complete meat-and-potatoes meal done with a flair to introduce flavors and nuances to heighten the pleasure of both food and wine. As it is comprised of varying elements, they are separately presented. (8 servings)

SAUCE
1/4 cup red wine (Caymus)
2 shallots, chopped
2-3 sprigs thyme
1 tablespoon sherry wine vinegar

1/2 cup chicken stock
1/3 cup veal stock
1 tablespoon butter
Salt and pepper

PARSNIP MASHED POTATOES
4-6 Idaho potatoes, peeled and cut into pieces
5 parsnips, peeled and cut into pieces
Cream (approximately 1 cup)
Salt and pepper
PARSNIP CHIPS
1-2 parsnips

1 tablespoon butter
SAUTÉED FIELD MUSHROOMS
12 ounces mushrooms, stem tips snipped, cut coarsely
1 tablespoon butter

Salt and pepper

8 8-ounce individual filets of beef

FOR THE SAUCE
1. In a saucepan, reduce the red wine, shallots and thyme until almost dry.
2. Add sherry wine vinegar, scraping the pan to incorporate caramelized remainders; add chicken and veal stocks and reduce by $1/3^{rd}$.
3. Swirl in butter, add salt and pepper, set aside and keep warm.
FOR THE PARSNIP MASHED POTATOES
1. In separate pots, cook potatoes and parsnips until tender.
2. Put both in food processor, blend while adding enough cream until smooth, and season with salt and pepper; set aside and keep warm.
FOR THE PARSNIP CHIPS (GARNISH)
Slice at a bias angle into oval coins, $1/8$" thick, fry in butter.
FOR THE SAUTÉED FIELD MUSHROOMS
Sauté in slightly-browned butter and season with salt and pepper. Set aside and keep warm.
TO ASSEMBLE
1. Grill the filets until medium-rare.
2. Put a large dollop of potato-parsnip melange on plates.
3. Place cooked filets on top of each.
4. Lightly nap with sauce, then add mushrooms on the side.
5. Garnish with fresh thyme and parsnip chips, and serve.

THE WINE WITH THIS RECIPE
...becomes much fuller, the tannins are accented, and the wine becomes opulent. The mouth feel enlarges, and propels the wine to an even higher level. The food, too, is enhanced by the wine, as its components, especially the earthy flavor the turnips bring to the party, gain much from this accompaniment. Definitely a great dinner wine and a great wine dinner.

CHATEAU
MONTELENA
1972 – 1992
ANNIVERSARY

THE MONTELENA ESTATE
Cabernet Sauvignon
NAPA VALLEY
1992
GROWN, PRODUCED & ESTATE BOTTLED BY
CHATEAU MONTELENA WINERY, CALISTOGA, CALIFORNIA
TABLE WINE

CHATEAU MONTELENA CABERNET SAUVIGNON

...has a dark red-brick color, deep and intense. There are splashes of cherries in the nose, along with tar and a hint of oak. The fruit caps off its good Cabernet aromas. There is clearly a powerful fruit and tannin structure, bold and assertive, a full-bodied, hearty taste. This is a gloriously big wine.

SERVE WITH
VENISON CHOPS MONTELENA

Winemaker Bo Barrett created this stimulating way of serving deer. The shallot and porcini sauce accent the earthiness of the meat remarkably well. Most good Italian delis stock porcini, oil-cured olives can be had from most Middle-Eastern grocery stores, and specialty butchers either have or can obtain venison—unless you are or know a good hunter, of course. The effort will be well worth it! (4-6 servings)

3-4 tablespoons dried ceps (porcini mushrooms)
2-3 shallots, minced
Olive oil or butter
2 cups beef, chicken or vegetable stock
2 tablespoons pitted and chopped oil-cured olives
Oregano and marjoram, fresh if available
4-6 venison chops (lamb chops can substitute)

1. Crumble ceps in non-metal bowl and cover with stock. Microwave 1-2 minutes to rehydrate.
2. Sauté shallots in a splash of olive oil or butter until translucent or caramelized, if you prefer. Add ceps, stock, olives, and a pinch each of the oregano and marjoram, continue to sauté, and reduce to sauce-like consistency. When ready, remove sauce from heat.
3. Cook chops over high heat, either broiled, pan fried, or barbecue grilled, but they are best brought to the table when hot and rare. Pour the sauce in a broad band across each chop, include some of the funghi and olives on each one, and serve.

THE WINE WITH THIS RECIPE

...smoothes into its flavors, its tannin structure excellently responding to the full flavors in the meal. The fruit qualities become more prominent, blackberry and cherry emerging, enveloping the tongue. The notes of olive in the meal shine with this wine, and the venison's pleasant earthiness, teamed with the qualities of the mushrooms, are elevated by this superb combination.

DIAMOND CREEK CABERNET SAUVIGNON
RED ROCK TERRACE

…features a deep red color, and provides a full Cabernet nose, hints of oak, and cherry. Full, robust mouth feel, excellent up front fruit, graceful and powerful as the flavors emerge; the structure is almost perfect.

SERVE WITH
FILET MIGNON, PEPPERED AND CHARBROILED, WITH PORTOBELLO MUSHROOM SAUCE, SERVED ON A BED OF JULIENNED VEGETABLES AND POTATO CAKE WITH ROASTED TOMATO

This complete meal recipe, masterminded by chef/owner Robert Bell of Chez Melange restaurant in Redondo Beach, California, is gloriously elaborate, the mushroom sauce requiring veal stock to be reduced to a brown stock to be reduced to a glace, delicate potato pancakes resting on top of a party of vegetables, a pepper-encrusted tenderloin, all tiered together, garnished by a tangy roasted Roma tomato. (4 servings)

4 8-ounce Filet Mignons
Cracked black peppercorns
VEGETABLES
1 each carrot, zucchini, crook-
   neck squash, red onion, red
   bell pepper, green bell pepper,
   julienne

1/4 cup olive oil
POTATO PANCAKES
3 medium-sized red potatoes,
   grated
1/2 yellow onion, grated
2 eggs, beaten
1/3 cup flour

1/3 cup sour cream
2 ounces milk
1 teaspoon thyme, chopped fine
Salt, pepper to taste

MUSHROOM SAUCE
2 cups red wine (Cabernet)
1 ounce shallots, diced fine
1 1/2 cups veal glace
2 portobello mushrooms, stems removed, cut into 1/4" cubes

1 teaspoon thyme, chopped fine
1 clove garlic, chopped fine
Salt and pepper to taste

ROASTED TOMATOES
4 Roma tomatoes, bottoms and tops removed
4 cloves of garlic, cut into slivers
1 teaspoon rosemary, finely chopped
Salt and pepper, to taste

TO MAKE POTATO PANCAKES
Mix all ingredients thoroughly, divide into fourths, make each into a pancake, cook on hot non-stick sauté pan. Set aside.

TO MAKE SAUCE
Reduce wine with shallots to 1/2 cup; add veal glace, reduce until thickened. Sauté mushrooms, thyme, and garlic until mushrooms are cooked, 5-6 minutes; add to sauce reduction, add salt and pepper to taste.

TO MAKE ROASTED TOMATOES
Stuff 3 pieces of slivered garlic into the tops of the tomatoes; sprinkle with rosemary, salt and pepper. Bake in 350°F oven 12 minutes. Serve hot.

TO SERVE
1. Encrust filet mignons with cracked black peppercorns.
2. Cook on grill until medium rare.
3. Sauté julienned vegetables in olive oil until onions are lightly clarified, add salt and pepper to taste.
4. Divide vegetables into fourths, spread each part out on a plate to size of pancake.
5. Heat potato pancakes in oven, place on top of vegetables.
6. Place meat on top of pancake, finish with sauce.
7. Garnish with roasted tomato.

THE WINE WITH THIS RECIPE
...has its boldness matched without giving an inch. The tannin structure holds up spectacularly, and the dark cherry in the wine emerges alongside the mushroom flavor. The vegetables draw out the hearty spice and pepper flavors in the wine, with the tomato adding just the right acid zest .

DUCKHORN VINEYARDS

1991
NAPA VALLEY
HOWELL MOUNTAIN
Merlot 49%, Cabernet Sauvignon 43%
Cabernet Franc 8%

DUCKHORN VINEYARDS
HOWELL MOUNTAIN RED

...is deep dark ruby red, with an opulent nose, with fruit of cassis, cherry and berry, and just a small touch of oak along with tobacco to present a clearly attractive nose. It provides a generous mouth feel, loads of sound tannins that complement the fruit elements stylishly. The fruit is full and strong, gently buffered by the Merlot and dosed with spice from the Cabernet Franc. Silky and bold at the same time, it continues its mastery of the mouth through its lasting finish. This wine has all the qualities that makes the name Duckhorn synonymous with expert "California Bordeaux."

SERVE WITH
FILET MIGNON FINALE

This is Hendrik Van Leuven's salute to Dan Duckhorn's remarkable wine. Amalgamating a recipe he discovered from a compilation of

Mary and Vincent Price's favorites, along with an au poivre inspiration of Trisha Volk and Mary Tartaglione from their *Signature Dishes* book, this creation employs some sleight of hand to pocket some paté within a filet before encrusting it with some ground green peppercorns. Cooking it "plug" side down first minimizes the threat of the heated paté oozing out. (4 servings)

4 8-12 ounce filets mignon, approximately 1 - 1^1/2" thick
^{1}/2 pound paté de foie gras
8 paper-thin slices of pancetta
Green peppercorns, freshly ground
Watercress

1. Working from about ^{1}/4" from the edge of each filet, cut an interior circle matching the circumference of the filet about half-way deep, then "bend" the meat's sides in order to cut this "plug" out.
2. Place a healthy portion of the paté into this cavity, then return the plug to its hole, pressing down gently but firmly to return it to its original level.
3. Wrap the pancetta around the outside of the disk of meat, one per half-circle, folded over if necessary.
4. Thoroughly dust both flat sides of the filet with the ground green peppercorns.
5. Barbecue on medium-hot coals until done, approximately 5-6 minutes per side, cooking "plug" side down first, being careful when turning not to let it pop out or lose it.
6. Serve garnished with light sprays of watercress.

THE WINE WITH THIS RECIPE
…becomes even more smooth and flavorful! The three wine components are well complemented by this recipe, the Cabernet Sauvignon by the meat and pepper, the soft Merlot to the mellow paté, and spicy Cabernet Franc by the truffles and pancetta. These are bold flavors, both in wine and food, and together they create fresh textures and eruptions, the wine engagingly cooling and soothing the conflagrations in the mouth. Bravo!

DUCKHORN VINEYARDS

1993
NAPA VALLEY
MERLOT

DUCKHORN VINEYARDS MERLOT

…features a medium brick color, and releases hints of spice, berries, cassis, cherries, simply great Merlot character. With its medium body weight, it is velvety in the mouth, loads of fruit, big, bold yet unquestionably elegant. As it provides a gloriously long finish, the total experience begins to gather in the mind and define itself as one of the finest examples of Merlot craftsmanship available.

SERVE WITH
GRILLED WILD DUCK WITH DUCKY'S WILD DUCK PORT SAUCE

Dan Duckhorn himself caught the culinary muse for this delicious way of making wild duck take flight. To the same extent that one might take stock and reduce reduce reduce in order to make a glace, Dan does the same thing with an entire bottle of port, along with some savory additions. If wild duck is a little hard to come by, try this with squab. (2+ servings)

SAUCE

1 bottle California Port (Ficklin's)
1 cup orange juice
1 lemon, juiced
2 cloves garlic, crushed
1 1/2 teaspoons Worcestershire sauce
4 teaspoons concentrated liquid
  beef bouillon (Bovril)
1 red onion, sliced thinly
2 slices of red or green bell pepper

2 heaping teaspoons Major Grey's
  peach chutney
4 heaping teaspoons blackberry
  seedless jam
Dash mixed herbs (thyme, marjoram, oregano)
Salt, pepper to taste
1/2 cup butter (chilled near freezing)

Wild ducks, 1/2 duck per person

FOR THE SAUCE

1. In a large sauce pan, bring entire bottle of port to a simmer; add orange and lemon juices, simmer for 15 minutes on medium heat.
2. Add garlic, Worcestershire sauce and bouillon; float slice of red onion and two pepper strips on top; add chutney, jam and mixed herbs; add salt and pepper to taste. Reduce sauce 50% over low heat.
3. Strain, then continue reduction over low heat until dark brown and syrupy.
4. At serving time, add dollops of butter, stirring until combined.

FOR THE DUCK

Grill the ducks using indirect heat (a la Weber Cookers), either on a rack or rotisserie, until done, or until the drumstick almost falls off the bone and the juices run clear.

TO SERVE

Slice duck, place on individual plates. Spoon sauce over duck and serve.

THE WINE WITH THIS RECIPE

…has its spiciness extracted with aplomb, the angles of the sauce sharpening all the flavors in the game to work with the fruit in the wine. This is a memorable experience, as the succulent gaminess of the duck, the diversities of the sauce, and the complexity of the wine, combine to make for an ideal meal.

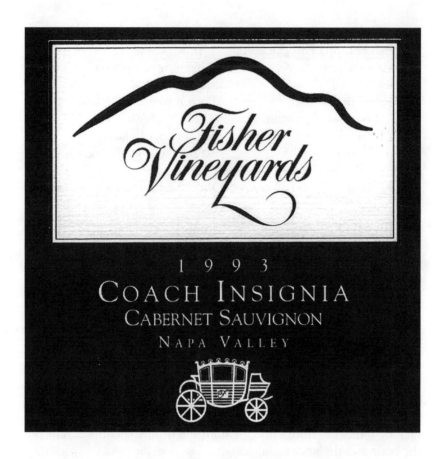

FISHER VINEYARDS CABERNET SAUVIGNON
COACH INSIGNIA

...has an alluring garnet color, with a full, luscious nose, touching on eucalyptus, cherries, and wood. There is full, fruit flavor in the mouth, all sorts of berries popping into the picture, along with a trace of tobacco. Its excellent long finish continues to tell you how good it is.

SERVE WITH
PICNIC LAMB KABOBS

The advance preparation, the marinade, makes for an astounding barbecue meal, flavorful, tender, and easy to serve. Juelle Fisher, co-owner of the winery, has a great way to turn a picnic into an elegant affair. (4 servings)

1 pound lamb, cut in 1" cubes
1/4 cup olive oil
1/4 cup Balsamic vinegar
3 tablespoons lemon juice
1 tablespoon oregano
1/2 cup chopped onion
2 garlic cloves, chopped
1/4 teaspoon salt
1/4 teaspoon ground pepper
Red bell peppers, cut into 3" pieces (optional)
French or pita bread

1. Place all ingredients except peppers and bread in a plastic zip lock bag and refrigerate for at least 3 days—it is absolutely worth the wait.
2. To cook, put lamb on skewers, alternating with peppers if desired. Barbecue over charcoal or mesquite to desired doneness.
3. Serve the lamb on French bread or, even better, with pita.

THE WINE WITH THIS RECIPE
…is simply incredible. The garlic and onion themes blend perfectly with the flavors of the wine, as does the Balsamic vinegar taste. The wine is grandly mellowed with its solid backbone still in place. This is truly a memorable, perfect match; it's as if they were meant for each other—and they are!

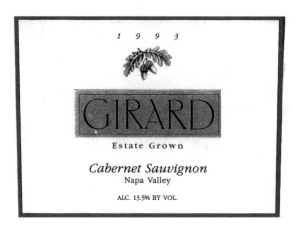

GIRARD WINERY CABERNET SAUVIGNON

...has an inviting garnet color, and its nose exhibits wonderful aromas of berries, cherries, and cassis, with a dash of oak. A very attractive and floral scent, it smells like a beautiful Cabernet. The mouth reveals wonderful richness and fullness with an excellent tannin structure. Flavors of cassis and fruit are joined with an inviting hint of eucalyptus, that wend their way through to the finish.

SERVE WITH

MIGNON OF GAME WITH PERSIMMON SAUCE

It's the sauce that makes this a most unique recipe, persimmons being one of the most challenging flavors possible. A fresh bite of this fruit simply occupies the mouth to such a degree that it feels like it's been coated with superglued velvet, upside-down. But as tempered here, it becomes lush, lusty, deep and appealing. A creation of chef Damon Brady from Bistro 45 in Pasadena, California, this was originally tabbed for elk, but venison or even lamb will do. (Fortunately, most game hunters who go after elk, antelope, moose, caribou, etc., do so for the opportunity to acquire exotic game meat for personal consumption and less for show; understandably, most tend to be willing to share with those who'd like to partake in viands otherwise unobtainable—in fact, they'll want your recipes!) Given that this is one of the most unique sauces ever, let your imagination take it into other meals of your own doing. (4 servings)

4 6-ounce filets of game meat
String for trussing
2 cups demi-glace
1 ounce fresh ginger
1 teaspoon dried ginger
1/2 cup panko (Japanese bread
  crumbs)

3 ripe persimmons
1 teaspoon sugar
1 shallot
1/2 cup red wine (Cabernet)
6 potatoes, peeled and quartered
Clarified butter
Salt and pepper, to taste

PREPARATION

1. Cut and tie the string around the mignons the short way, creating little "bales," then set aside.
2. Place bread crumbs in food processor with both gingers, pulse until all are incorporated; set aside.
3. Roast the persimmons for 2 1/2 minutes in a 450°F oven or until soft. Let slightly cool, then scrape out the meat and purée in a food processor; set aside.
4. Cook potatoes in water until soft, puéee in food processor with salt, pepper, and clarified butter, then form into 3" round patties, and refrigerate.

TO ASSEMBLE

1. Sear the potato patties in a non-stick pan, set aside, keep warm.
2. Caramelize the sugar in a 2-quart sauce pan, add persimmon purée, quickly add wine and reduce by half; add demi-glace and reduce slightly, then season to taste.
3. Sear off venison in a hot pan, then roast until rare.
4. Cutting the string free, place each piece on a potato cake, ladle sauce around edge and on top of venison.
5. Just prior to serving, dust meat with the panko-ginger powder, and with or without desired vegetable brown it in the oven.

THE WINE WITH THIS RECIPE

...increases its scope delightfully. The flavor of the persimmon heightens the complexity of the wine, as the tannins conjoin with the "puckery" fruit. Further, the sweetness of the sauce considerably deepens the fruit in the wine, making this one of the most unusual and soothing flavor combinations possible.

GRGICH HILLS CABERNET SAUVIGNON

…features a deep, rich red color, and provides a full Cabernet nose, with wisps of cassis, berries, tobacco and tar, a most inviting earthy character. In the mouth, it is comfortably tannic, and its wealth of fruit is touched with an alluring pepper structure. Bold, assertive, assured, its completing finish secures this as a decidedly well-crafted wine.

SERVE WITH
PAN-ROASTED RIBEYE STEAK WITH WINE SAUCE

Restaurateur Robert Gadsby was kind enough to craft this recipe to accompany this fine wine. The creative touch of using bone marrow as an accompaniment to the red wine and shallot sauce adds a unique consistency to each bite.

RED WINE SAUCE	6 ounce ribeye steaks, 1 per person
4 shallots, finely chopped	1-2 tablespoons vegetable oil
1 1/4 cups red wine (Grgich)	1 ounce unsalted butter
1/2 cup port	24 pieces marrow bone
1 cup poultry stock	Salt, crushed white pepper
2 oz. diced unsalted butter	

FOR THE SAUCE

1. Marinate the shallots in 1/4 cup each of the wine and port for 24 hours.
2. Pour remaining wine and port into a saucepan, bring to a boil, and reduce by one-half, or until it has a light sauce consistency.
3. In another pan, bring the stock to a boil and continue to simmer until reduced by 3/4s or until it coats the back of a spoon.
4. Add the wine reduction to the stock, add the butter, and swirl to combine.
5. Simmer the shallots and marinade until it has almost evaporated, then add to the wine sauce just before serving.

TO PREPARE STEAKS

1. Pan-fry the steaks in hot oil for 3 minutes per side, depending on the thickness; when the steaks are cooked, remove them from the pan and allow to set for 5 minutes.
2. Bring a small pot of salted water to a boil. Add marrow bones. Cook for 2 minutes, then drain off water and remove the marrow (they should "pop" out and retain their disk-like shapes). Set aside.

TO SERVE

Place each steak on a plate, topping each with 2-3 marrow pieces. Pour some sauce over and around each steak, season with salt and pepper, and serve.

THE WINE WITH THIS RECIPE

…has its strengths heartily directed, becoming richer and bolder, yet maintaining the pleasant attractions from its tannins. The fruit becomes more prevalent, the cassis reacting beautifully with the port tones in the sauce, and the pepperiness in the wine is elicited by the meat. The intriguing marrow lends a creaminess to the feel and cushions the earth in the wine.

NAPA VALLEY
CABERNET SAUVIGNON
ALCOHOL 13½% BY VOLUME

PRODUCED AND BOTTLED IN OUR CELLAR BY
HEITZ WINE CELLARS
ST. HELENA, CALIFORNIA, U.S.A.

HEITZ CELLAR CABERNET SAUVIGNON
MARTHA'S VINEYARD

...features a deep, dark red color, and presents incredible fruit in the nose, with hints of peppermint and herbs, a good smell of oak and earth. It is thoroughly full-bodied in the mouth, expressing classic tannin structure; great flavors of fruit, tobacco, cherry, cassis, all balanced with the tannins.

SERVE WITH
VEAL LUISA

This variation on the Italian classic was crafted at Piero Selvaggio's Los Angeles restaurant Valentino. The mushrooms' earthiness, the ham's piquancy and the medium of the veal are delicious vehicles to transport this wine to fresh levels of enjoyment. (6 servings)

2 ounces porcini (dry)
3 shallots, chopped
1 clove garlic, chopped
1 small onion, chopped
2 tablespoons butter
4 tablespoons oil
1 teaspoon thyme, finely chopped
5 ounces dry Marsala
5 ounces whipping cream

Salt, pepper
12 scallopine of veal
2 eggs, beaten
3 teaspoons all-purpose flour
12 pieces thin, sliced ham (matching size of veal)
12 slices mozzarella cheese
1/8 cup dry white wine
24 slices pimiento (optional)

1. Soak porcini mushrooms in tepid water for 1/2 hour. Drain, chop.
2. Sauté shallots, onion and garlic in 1 tablespoon butter and 2 tablespoons oil until clear.
3. Add chopped mushrooms, 1 tablespoon flour and mix well.
4. Add Marsala, whipping cream, salt and pepper to taste, and cook 2-3 minutes. Set aside for final assembly.
5. Dust veal with remaining flour.
6 Dip in egg and sauté in pan with 1 tablespoon butter and 2 tablespoons oil, 1 minute per side.
7. Sprinkle with thyme and remove from heat, leaving flame on.
8. With the veal in the pan, top each scallopine with 1 heaping tablespoon of the reserved mushroom stuffing. Top each with a slice of ham and slice of cheese.
9. Add white wine to the pan and return to heat.
10. Top each with pimiento, cover pan and cook over medium heat 1 minute, or until cheese melts. Serve immediately.

THE WINE WITH THIS RECIPE

...becomes altogether elegant, together quite a production. The porcini indeed makes the flavors of the fruit in the wine emerge all the more triumphant, then they step aside to let the other complexities take their turn, none so demanding to become over-assertive, but working in pairs, in threes, more, they become a company, the wine and the dish, to produce magic. Each bite, each sip, finishes with a flourish, the beautiful mint comes out, is joined by the thyme, the wine leaves traces of its glory, and there is nothing left to do but...encore!

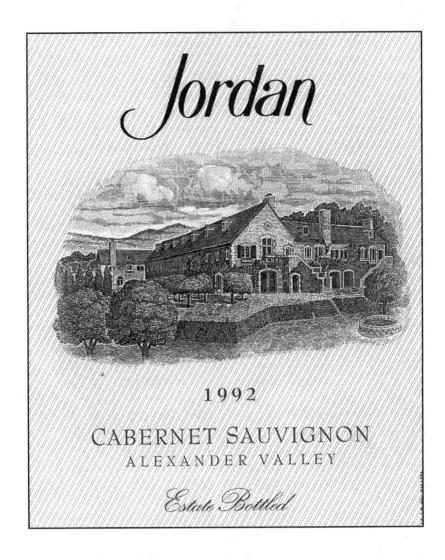

JORDAN CABERNET SAUVIGNON

…has a deep ruby red color. Its nose features enticements of eucalyptus, tobacco, tar, and oak, with a slight hint of berry—it smells like a Cabernet should. It features a feel-good medium voluptuousness in the mouth, its berry character emerging nicely. It's completed with a lush, smooth finish, making it an enormously drinkable wine.

SERVE WITH
MARINATED CALIFORNIA GOAT CHEESE

For a mid-meal dash of excitement or as a finishing touch to a heady dinner, this strong-flavored cheese creation can exhilarate your palate to fresh flights of fancy. It is memorable and somewhat addictive! Because it's a long-term marinade, you can aim for a particular date or keep some on hand for whenever the urge strikes, knowing that it can last for months. This comes from the winery itself, whose Chef de Cuisine, Thomas Oden, agrees the wonders of this recipe last and last and last.

6 small goat cheeses or cheese portions, which have been aged a minimum of 10 days. (Fresh goat cheese will absorb too much oil. We used cheese that had been aged for over 365 days; it worked fine!)
2 cloves garlic, peeled
6 black peppercorns, whole
2 small, dried chili peppers
2 sage leaves
3 sprigs thyme
1 sprig rosemary
1 bay leaf
Top quality extra virgin olive oil

Put all ingredients in a jar, cover with olive oil, secure the lid, and marinate at cellar temperature or in the refrigerator for a week or longer. If refrigerated, bring the cheese to room temperature before serving. Spoon several tablespoons of the olive oil from the jar over the cheese and decorate with a small quantity of the herbs from the marinade. Serve with roasted bell peppers, a green salad, or fresh bread, such as pita or French.

THE WINE WITH THE RECIPE
...has its fruitiness accented, its berriness pushed forward with most edifying results. It's a very different dish, but provides a joyous robustness with this smooth, classy Cabernet. The wine keeps providing, opening, and is clearly exquisite with this full-bodied cheese. The only concern will be which runs out first!

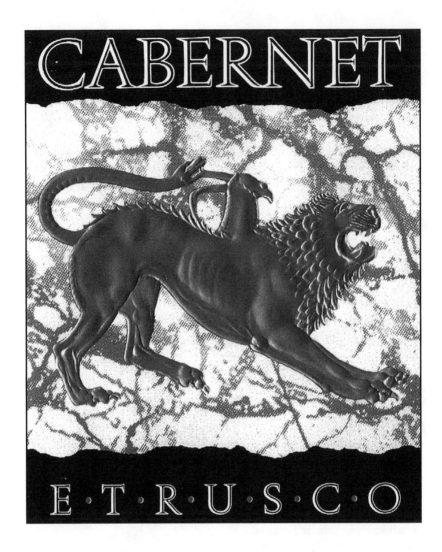

MARTIN BROS. WINERY
CABERNET ETRUSCO

...has a medium-red color, and the nose provides engaging wisps of fruit, almost floral, cleverly aromatic without being burdensome. There is noticeable spice in the mouth, full, bright and flavorful, thanks to the Sangiovese, with the Cabernet contribution comfortably subtle to balance it off. Hand in hand, they carry through into the finish, a most satisfying culmination.

New York Steaks with Wild Mushroom Ragout

The fabulous Pasadena, California, restaurant Bistro 45 and chef Kei-ji Mizukami provided this relatively simple way to enjoy a fine steak and sauce with a fine bottle of wine. (4 servings)

4 teaspoons butter
5 shallots, chopped
1 pound wild mushrooms (shiitake, oyster, portobello, Paris), sliced
1 cup sherry
1 cup veal stock
1/4 cup cream
2 teaspoons chopped parsley
Salt, pepper
4 8-ounce New York steaks

1. Melt butter in large pan. Add shallots, and sauté until tender.
2. Add mushrooms, cook, occasionally stirring, for 6 minutes.
3. Add sherry and stock, and boil until liquid is reduced by half.
4. Add cream and parsley, and boil about 2 minutes. Season with salt and pepper.
5. Grill the steaks to your liking, and serve them with the sauce.

The wine with this recipe
...collects its due from the two basic elements, mushroom and meat, and pushes things up and out. The Sangiovese finds the mushrooms and creates a small whirlpool, the Cabernet does the same with the steak, and with the sauce acting as a binding agent, the mouth enjoys quite a confluence of forces. A simple, superb combination.

LOUIS M. MARTINI CABERNET SAUVIGNON
RESERVE

…has a beautiful red-purple color. The nose features good fruit characteristics, tones of ripe berry, tobacco, and cassis, with a pleasing touch of oak. There is a robust feel in the mouth, excellent tannin structure, fulfilling the flavors first found in the nose. With its secure finish, this is truly a substantial wine.

SERVE WITH
SPAGHETTINI PRIMAVERA

Elizabeth Martini's files are a veritable storehouse for fine meals to go with their fine wines. This recipe, pure spring in its outlook, combines rusticity with elegance, and explodes with flavor. (4 servings)

1 pound Italian sausage, hot
1 pound Italian spaghettini
4 tablespoons olive oil
$^1/_2$ lb. Chinese pea pods, strings removed, chilled in ice water
2 cloves garlic, finely minced
$^1/_2$ pound zucchini, young and tender, thinly sliced
1 can (28 ounces) Italian plum tomatoes, drained and chopped

$1^1/_4$ cups fresh parsley, chopped
1 sprig fresh oregano (or 1 tea-spoon dried)
$^1/_4$ cup fresh basil, chopped
3 red bell peppers, thinly sliced
$1^1/_4$ cups Parmesan cheese, freshly grated
Salt, fresh ground pepper
French bread

1. Cover sausages in water, boil until cooked (about 30 minutes). Remove, peel, and thinly slice.
2. Heat 2 tablespoons oil in heavy skillet over medium heat. Add sausage, increase heat to medium-high, thoroughly brown sausage. Remove.
3. Discard all but 2 tablespoons fat from skillet. Tone down heat, add garlic and sauté until transparent (not brown). Add tomatoes, 1 cup of parsley, oregano, salt and pepper. Cover and simmer gently 15 minutes; watch carefully and stir occasionally (add water, stock or wine if it becomes too dry). Add sausage, cover and keep warm.
4. Cook spaghettini in boiling, slightly salted and lightly oiled water until done while sauce is being completed.
5. In another skillet or wok pan, add the remaining 2 tablespoons oil and heat to medium-high. Dry the snow peas on paper towels. Add the zucchini and red bell peppers to the skillet and sauté a few minutes, then add the snow peas and cook until they turn a bright green.
6. Pasta done, drain and place in a large bowl; sprinkle with the basil.
7. Add the vegetables to the sauce, then completely pour over the pasta and toss thoroughly.
8. Add the remaining parsley and $^3/_4$ cup Parmesan, reserving the remaining cheese for those who wish more.

THE WINE WITH THIS RECIPE
...actually mellows a bit, while standing up to the exciting flavors in the meal, bursting with black pepper accents. The green peppers, peas and sausage highlight the qualities of this wine, stimulating its fruit in the mouth.

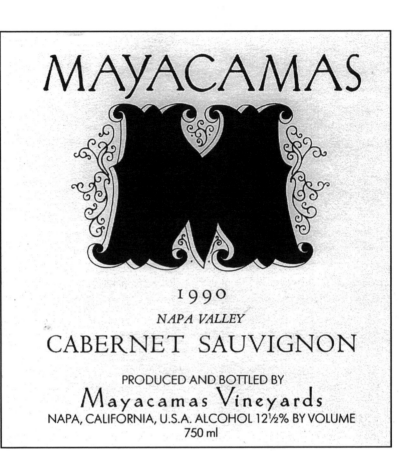

MAYACAMAS VINEYARDS CABERNET SAUVIGNON
...has a deep red hue, with huge tones of berry, tobacco, tar, and cassis in the nose. The mouth feel is...WOW, great fruit, leather, full-bodied Cabernet character, simply a tremendous wine.

Beef Tenderloin

This is a three-part method of cooking beef that locks in flavor not once but twice, and after stage two can be refrigerated until ready to complete the process. It comes from Nonie Travers, co-owner of the winery, and is proof that mountain living can produce wonders.

As many 6-to-8 ounce tenderloins as there are people to be served
2 cloves garlic, crushed, for every 4 steaks
Butter
Salt and pepper

1. Sauté tenderloins in butter with garlic, salt and pepper, until completely, lightly browned.
2. Broil the meat 10-12 minutes on each side, then either refrigerate or proceed to final phase.
3. Bake at 350°F for 20-30 minutes, depending on how rare desired. Serve and slice.

The wine with this recipe
…makes bold, sweeping statements of flavor. There is smoothness, excellent fruit, with a slightly jammy quality that pleases the palate. The tannins take note of the garlic, making it prevalent yet subtle. This is a perfect match for those who like huge flavors that fly like the Valkyrie!

1991

OPUS ONE

A NAPA VALLEY
RED WINE

PRODUCED AND
BOTTLED BY

ROBERT MONDAVI

BARON PHILIPPE DE ROTHSCHILD

OAKVILLE, CALIFORNIA
PRODUCT OF USA
CONTAINS SULFITES
750 ML/75.0 CL
ALCOHOL 13.5% BY VOLUME
© RMR COMPANY 1983

OPUS ONE

...looks great in the glass, a dark, rich red. Swirling it around releases currant, dark cherries, hints of oak—it lifts its eyebrows alluringly, suavely. Rolling around the tongue, it laughs—great character, a touch of spice, the fruit is solidly defined, and the puzzles of its personality fit perfectly together. Swallow, it spreads its wealth into the throat, luxuriates there, and smiles assuredly, coyly, as it fades away into the walls of memory. A great red wine.

SERVE WITH
GRILLED LAMB WITH BLACK CURRANTS

A meal from Michael's Restaurant in Santa Monica, California, is a consistent pleasure, and this contribution is no exception. This recipe has an original pedigree that stretches back to the founder of the Pepperidge Farm baking company, Martha Rudkin, passed on to her son Mark, then to Michael McCarty himself, and now to you. Although it originally calls for an entire saddle of lamb, which when deboned produces two 10 ounce loins and two 3 ounce tenderloins, it's been slightly modified here to accommodate 1 1/2 pounds of lamb tenderloins regardless of how acquired. It's recommended that the fire be searing hot, in order to char the red currant coating into a glaze, and for those who truly enjoy a red rare hunk of lamb, this is a sweetly flavorful way to enjoy it—and with a masterful wine to boot. (4 servings)

1-1 1/2 pounds lamb tenderloin, cut into four portions
1/2 cup red currant jelly, melted

1 1/2 CUPS CABERNET CASSIS SAUCE
3/4 cup Opus One
1/4 cup black currants
2 tablespoons cassis syrup
2 cups poultry or lamb stock (see Appendix B)

1 clove double-blanched garlic*
2 fresh basil leaves
1 teaspoon chilled unsalted butter
Salt, freshly ground white pepper
3/4 cup fresh or frozen black currants

1 tablespoon fresh tarragon leaves, lightly chopped
1 teaspoon fresh thyme leaves, lightly chopped

To prepare lamb

Brush the lamb liberally with the red currant jelly and leave it to marinate for about 30 minutes at room temperature.

To make the sauce

1. In a small, heavy, non-aluminum saucepan, boil the Cabernet with the black currants and cassis syrup over high heat until the liquid has reduced by three quarters to a thick syrup, approx. 5-7 minutes.
2. Add the stock and simmer on medium heat, skimming the surface frequently if necessary, until the sauce is thick enough to coat the back of a spoon and has reduced to about 1^1/2 cups, about 10-15 minutes.
3. Add the blanched garlic (see below) and basil, and swirl in the butter until thoroughly incorporated.
4. Strain the sauce through a fine-mesh sieve, and return it to the pan to warm through gently. Season to taste with salt and pepper.
5. Add the 3/4 cup of black currants, heat through, and keep the sauce warm.

* To double-blanch garlic, place peeled clove in small pan, cover with cold water and bring to boil. Drain water, fill again with cold water, bring to boil, and drain once more. Use whole or cut into eighths.

To cook and serve lamb

1. Preheat grill or boiler until very hot.
2. Grill the lamb, about 3-4 minutes per side for medium-rare—at the halfway point through cooking on each side, rotate the meat 90 degrees to give it cross-hatched grill marks. (Note: If there are those who want their lamb cooked more substantially, butterfly at this point and similarly cook until finished.)
3. Carve the lamb into 1/4" slices and arrange on heated serving plates.
4. Spoon the sauce with the black currants on top.
5. Garnish with a sprinkling of the fresh tarragon and thyme.

THE WINE WITH THIS RECIPE

...is a complete theatrical experience. All that is active in the wine becomes accented by the recipe—spices are freshened, the currants and fruit are heightened, the finish gains fresh perspective. The meal, too, has its qualities elevated—it is somehow rough and delicate at the same time, not unlike the wine, a complete yin-yang involvement. It comes together.

RIDGE CABERNET SAUVIGNON
MONTE BELLO

...features an intense red-purple color, and the nose instantly bursts with aromas, full berry character, cassis, cherries, with oak lurking delightfully about. It entertains the palate in the mouth with further embellishments of its flavors, along with earth and pepper, a statement of oak, and simply laden with fruit. With its long finish keeping its impact alive well beyond reason, this superb wine is flat-out fantastic.

SERVE WITH
PEPPERED ROAST LAMB LOIN WITH VEGETABLE PANACHE

This recipe comes from restaurateur Robert Gadsby, and was tailored specifically for this wine. It employs lamb stock from which a brown sauce emerges, and when combined with the full flavors of the meat along with the splashes of flavors from the disparate vegetables he's chosen, this becomes a very interesting, savory dish indeed. (4 servings)

LAMB SAUCE
5 pounds lamb bones
2 tablespoons vegetable oil
1 onion
1 celery stalk
1 leek
2 1/2 tablespoons tomato paste

11 cups water
3^1/$_2$ cups chicken stock
1 bay leaf
1 thyme sprig

CONFIT OF GARLIC
12-16 large garlic cloves
1 ounce olive oil
2 bay leaves
2 thyme sprigs
8 ounces warm water
Pinch of salt and pepper
Dash sugar

4 8-ounce lamb loins
Salt, freshly ground pepper
3^1/$_2$ ounces vegetable oil
1 ounce unsalted butter

8 baby fennel bulbs, trimmed
12 baby leeks, trimmed
12 thin asparagus spears
12 baby carrots
2 ounces unsalted butter
Dash sugar

2 fresh mint sprigs
Thyme sprigs

FOR THE LAMB SAUCE
1. Chop the lamb bones very finely, then roast them in 1 tablespoon of the oil in a roasting tray on the stove until golden brown, then drain the oil.
2. Clean and chop the vegetables into rough pieces. Sweat them in the remaining oil on the stove, then add the tomato paste and the bones.
3. Bring the water and stock to a boil in a separate pan, then pour over the bones and vegetables.

4. Bring the combined bones and stock to a boil, and skim the fat that rises.

5. Add the herbs, and cook at a fast simmer, skimming regularly, until reduced to about 5 cups. Divide in half, saving the balance for other use.

6. Pass sauce for the meal through a sieve or cheesecloth until liquid is completely clear.

FOR THE CONFIT

1. Heat the olive oil in a small saucepan, and sweat off the cloves until golden brown. Add the bay and thyme leaves.

2. Season with salt and add a dash of sugar.

3. Add the water and simmer gently until garlic cloves are tender to the touch.

TO PREPARE LAMB

1. Preheat the oven to 425°F.

2. Season the loins with salt and pepper, then pan-fry in an oven-proof pan in the oil, adding the butter during the cooking.

3. Place the pan in the oven and cook approximately 15 minutes (for medium rare); place under broiler for an additional 5 minutes, if desired, to ensure doneness.

4. Remove the pan from the oven and let rest for about 5-10 minutes.

TO SERVE

1. Cook the fennel, leeks and asparagus separately in boiling salted water until just before softening, then refresh in iced water.

2. Cook the carrots in 1 ounce of the butter, with a pinch each of salt and sugar, and a little water. Allow an emulsion to form around them.

3. Pan-fry the prepared garlic cloves in a dry pan until just crisp.

4. Reheat the green vegetables in boiling water, then roll them through an emulsion of the remaining butter and hot water.

5. Heat the lamb sauce gently, adding the freshly chopped mint leaves at the last minute.

6. Cut the lamb into thin slices (approximately 10 slices per loin), arrange on the plate in a semi-circle. Arrange the vegetables haphazardly over the lamb, then pour the minted lamb sauce all around,

with the thyme as a final garnish.

THE WINE WITH THIS RECIPE

...incredibly becomes even more intriguing. From the gaminess of the lamb it has its fruit expanded, from the roast nuttiness in the mild garlic confit its spice is enhanced, and from the vegetables its earthiness is celebrated. The wine is so full and round and luscious, its many layers flipping through the mouth, and this recipe's matching complexities positively pushing it to greater degrees of excitement, this is a supreme pairing of mind and matter.

1993
NAPA VALLEY
CABERNET SAUVIGNON
RESERVE
UNFILTERED
ROBERT MONDAVI WINERY

ROBERT MONDAVI WINERY CABERNET SAUVIGNON
RESERVE

…is deep, dark red and exudes a rich Cabernet nose, hints of tobacco and eucalyptus, with an intense sense of cassis and dark cherry. It provides an incredible mouth feel, immediately proving to be an accessible, inviting wine. The oak emerges, the tobacco is huge and lovely, and hidden in the back is a fling of bittersweet chocolate.

SERVE WITH
VEAL CHOPS CHASSEUR

Judy Breitstein has been involved in the wine-and-food matching process for almost 30 years as the co-owner of the Duke of Bourbon wine shop in Canoga Park, California. This is one of her favorites with this wine, and now we can taste why. What's convenient about it is that it can be prepared somewhat in advance, set aside, and re-heated just before serving. (6 servings)

6 large veal loin chops, 1" thick
2 tablespoons butter
1 tablespoon oil (more, if needed)
Salt, pepper
TOMATO-MUSHROOM SAUCE
3 tablespoons butter (if needed)
1/4 cup minced shallots
3/4 pound firm, ripe red toma-
toes, peeled, seeded, juiced and chopped (makes approximately 1 cup of pulp)

1/2 clove crushed garlic
Salt, pepper
1/2 teaspoon basil, minced
1/2 cup dry white wine (or 1/3

cup dry Vermouth)
1/2 cup brown sauce (or 1/2
    brown stock or canned
    beef boullion with 1
    tablespoon arrowroot or
    cornstarch, blended with

1 tablespoon water)
    1/2 lb. sliced fresh mushrooms
    2 tablespoons butter
    1 tablespoon oil
    2 tablespoons fresh, minced
      parsley

FOR THE CHOPS
1. Wash and dry the chops on paper towels.
2. Heat butter and oil in a large sauté pan until butter foam has almost subsided, then brown chops, two or three at a time, for 3-4 min. each side.
3. As they are done, season with salt and pepper and arrange in a large fireproof casserole dish, overlapping them slightly.

FOR THE TOMATO-MUSHROOM SAUCE
1. Pour all but 3 tablespoons of fat out of the sauté pan; if the fat has burned, pour it all out and add butter.
2. Stir in the shallots and cook slowly for 1 minute.
3. Stir in tomatoes, garlic, seasonings and herbs. Cover and simmer 5 min.
4. Pour in the wine and brown sauce (or the stock and corn starch). Boil rapidly 4-5 minutes, until the sauce has reduced and thickened.
5. Correct seasonings and remove from heat.
6. In a separate skillet, sauté mushrooms in butter and oil to brown lightly.
7. Season to taste and scrape them into the tomato sauce.
8. Return pan to heat, and simmer 1 minute, and correct seasoning again.

TO SERVE
1. Pour tomato-mushroom sauce over chops in the casserole, basting them. If not to be served immediately, set aside.
2. Shortly before serving, cover the casserole and reheat for 4-5 mintues without simmering.
3. Arrange the chops on a warm platter and pour sauce over.
4. Sprinkle with minced parsley.

THE WINE WITH THIS RECIPE
…becomes even more inviting and accessible. The acid from the tomato enjoys the encounter with the tannins, and the mushrooms bring out a most attractive and pleasing earthiness in the wine. A delectable drinking wine turns into a welcome companion with this veal—pull up a chair!

1993

NAPA VALLEY
CABERNET SAUVIGNON

Kara's Vineyard

BOTTLED AT THE CHÂTEAU

UNFILTERED

Robert Pecota
PROPRIETOR

ALC. 12.5 % BY VOL.

75 cl   PRODUCT OF U.S.A.

ROBERT PECOTA CABERNET SAUVIGNON
KARA'S VINEYARD

…has a fine, dark ruby glow in the glass, with a fruit-full nose, berry and cherry. In the mouth, the black cherry banks off a bit of vanilla, creating a smooth, rich mouth feel, with lovely balance. As a coda, a trace of tamarind is introduced as it fades into the later stages of its finish.

SERVE WITH
FLANK STEAK MARINADE

This is one of the most consistently fine ways of preparing flank steak, grill-in and grill-out. A creation of Susan Pecota, Kara Pecota Dunn's mother, this has been a family favorite for several years, and for very good reason: it is tender, juicy, sumptuous, and pairs up with the Robert Pecota Cabernet Sauvignon beautifully. It's just about a perfect patio or picnic main course. (4+ servings)

^{1}/4 cup soy sauce
3 tablespoons honey
2 tablespoons vinegar
1^1/2 teaspoons garlic, pressed
1^1/2 teaspoons ground ginger
1 yellow onion, sliced thinly
^{1}/2 -^{3}/4 cup salad oil
Flank steak (^{1}/2 pound per person)

Combine the above ingredients, place in a plastic bag or container, and marinate the meat overnight.

Barbecue the steak over high heat charcoals or mesquite, turning until completely cooked. Thinly slice against the grain into strips, serve.

THE WINE WITH THIS RECIPE
...seems to meld with the flavors in the marinade, which accents the fruit, engages the tannins, the soy and honey brightens the berry, and the ginger draws more of the tamarind out. There is joy in the simplicity of the meal greeting the elegance of the wine and finding they team up well—sometimes stealing moments to relax and enjoy nature's finest eases the stress from many of life's exigencies.

ROBERT PECOTA MERLOT
STEVEN ANDRE VINEYARD

...is nicely dark and ruby-colored. There is good, intense fruit in the nose, lots of spice, of cherries, concepts swirling around the interior of the glass. It provides a round, well-balanced mouth feel, lively in its proffering. The finish does not give up easily, as it slurs the persistent flavors together. This is a solidly well-made Merlot.

SERVE WITH
GRILLED LEG OF LAMB PECOTA

Another winner from the Pecota kitchen! The thick pepper-accented marinade works best the longer you leave it on, so it's best to prepare this the night before so it has ample time to work its wonders. (4 servings)

$1/2$ cup red Napa Valley wine (Robert Pecota)
1 cup garlic cloves
$1/4$ cup fresh rosemary leaves
1 tablespoon whole black peppercorns
2 teaspoons salt
1 cup olive oil
1 leg of lamb, butterflied, boneless

1. Combine wine, garlic, rosemary, pepper and salt in blender or food processor. Blend for approximately 30 seconds.
2. Slowly drizzle in the olive oil until an almost thick paste is created.
3. Place lamb in a large sealable plastic sack or bowl. Marinate the lamb in the refrigerator for 8-24 hours.
4. Grill the lamb on a barbecue until the meat reaches an internal temperature of 145-155°F, let stand for 15 minutes, carve and serve.

THE WINE WITH THIS RECIPE
…becomes dazzling, as the intensity of the flavors from the lamb, rosemary and garlic mesh with the fruit of the wine most adroitly. There's almost a pinball effect, as the flavors bounce up here, light up there, all the while the wine stays in play. The only thing that will tilt is your glass. Definitely a bonus match.

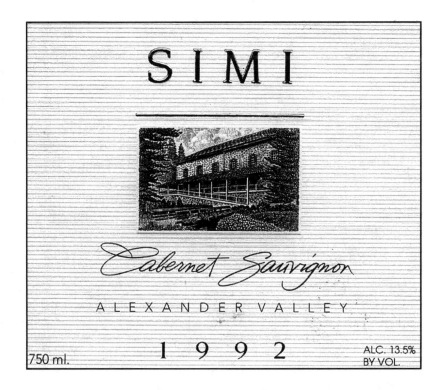

SIMI WINERY CABERNET SAUVIGNON

...enjoys a deep purple hue, with an excellent Cabernet nose, revealing scents of eucalyptus, and coyly hiding cigar tobacco (not too heavy), and showing fine fruit. In the mouth, excellently soft tannins are nicely balanced with a good fruit feel, with the tobacco definitely emerging triumphant and deepening itself into the finish.

SERVE WITH
BLACK OLIVE PESTO PIZETTE

A fun way to create mini-pizzas that can be made as presented— matched perfectly as they are with Simi's wines by their chef Mary Evely—or as platforms for your own culinary creativity. Plus, there's a little of the pesto leftover for use on sandwiches, pasta, or more pizette.

2 cans pitted black olives
2 cloves garlic, peeled
2 tablespoons pine nuts
1/2 cup olive oil
3/4 cup grated Asiago cheese
1 package (2 small sheets) frozen puff pastry
   (or make a standard pizza dough)

1. While the pastry defrosts, drain the olives, cut half of them into slices, place in small bowl and reserve.
2. Process garlic and pine nuts with steel blade until fine; add whole olives, cheese and oil, and puree. Fold pesto mix into the reserved sliced olives.
3. Preheat oven to 450°F.
4. Cut pastry into 16 rounds, place on lightly greased baking sheet. Spread olive pesto over the center of each round.
5. Bake for 15 minutes, or until pastry edges are browned.

THE WINE WITH THIS RECIPE
...is utterly transformed! The fruit explodes as the wine softens and smoothes out, bringing with it a full mouth feel. The olive flavors bring out a lovely huskiness from the tannins, and is carried into the finish. The rusticity of the flavors, the fun of the crumbly bulls-eye hors d'oeuvres, the heft of the wine, makes for a most enjoyable match.

SPOTTSWOODE

1992
CABERNET SAUVIGNON
Napa Valley

SPOTTSWOODE CABERNET SAUVIGNON

...features a dark purple color. The cassis in the nose is joined by wisps of cherries, berries, and subtleties of tobacco. Even more is revealed in the mouth, a classic tannin structure coupled with the fruit and a soupçon of oak, as all the flavors whisk around explosively, turning into an enduring finish that maintains the wondrous effect with confidence.

SERVE WITH
POLENTA E RAGU DI SELVAGGINA
(POLENTA WITH RABBIT AND GAME BIRDS STEW)

A game-infused recipe that calls for two kinds of fowl and some rabbit, this is a stew-oriented dish served on Polenta, which is prepared in the last five minutes of this relatively quick and easy production. It comes from the kitchen of the Los Angeles restaurant Valentino, intended specifically for this wine. (6 servings)

1/2 onion, chopped
1 carrot, julienne
2 celery sticks, julienne
1/4 cup olive oil
3 quails, boned, cut in half
2 squabs, boned, cut in 4 pieces
4 rabbit legs, cut in half
1 teaspoon fresh thyme, chopped
1 teaspoon fresh sage, chopped
1/2 cup red wine

1 quart brown stock
1 cup chicken broth
1/4 pound fresh porcini or shi-
    itake mushrooms
Salt & pepper
1 1/2 quarts of water
2 teaspoons plus 4 ounces butter
12 ounces of instant polenta
    (corn meal)

TO PREPARE RAGU

1. Sauté onion, carrot, celery sticks in deep frying pan with oil until brown.
2. Add the meat, and continue cooking until they begin coloring.
3. Add thyme and sage, and slowly sprinkle in red wine, cook until the color increases.
4. Pour in brown stock and chicken broth, cover, and simmer for 20 min.
5. Add mushrooms, cook for 10 minutes more. Salt and pepper to taste.
6. Let it simmer for about 20 minutes with covered lid, then add mushrooms and cook for 10 more minutes. Salt and pepper to taste.

TO PREPARE POLENTA

1. Bring the water to a boil.
2. Add 2 teaspoons butter, then the Polenta. Stir with a wooden spoon for about 5 minutes, or until it thickens.
3. Add 4 ounces of butter for extra flavor.

TO COMPLETE THE DISH

Having prepared the Polenta in the last 5 minutes while cooking the meats, as soon as it is ready place a portion on each plate, add samples of all the meats and sprinkle a generous portion of the sauce on top.

THE WINE WITH THIS RECIPE

…conducts the orchestra of flavors in the stew with an assured feel. The complexities of the wine more than handle the diversity that the meal entails, especially the tannins as they control and enhance the obtuse gamey qualities in the rabbit and birds. This most unusual meal blends well together, earth-to-earth, and the wine is extremely enjoyable because of it.

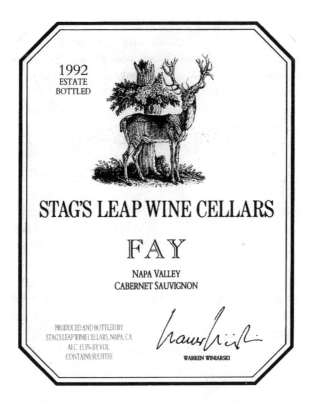

1992
ESTATE
BOTTLED

STAG'S LEAP WINE CELLARS

FAY

NAPA VALLEY
CABERNET SAUVIGNON

PRODUCED AND BOTTLED BY
STAG'S LEAP WINE CELLARS, NAPA, CA
ALC. 13.5% BY VOL.
CONTAINS SULFITES

WARREN WINIARSKI

STAG'S LEAP WINE CELLARS CABERNET SAUVIGNON
FAY

…is medium-dark red with a wonderful Cabernet nose, showing attractive notes of tar, tobacco, a medium cherry tone, and some oak, a full, complex nose. There is great up front fruit and splendid balance in the mouth and throughout, it totally fills the senses on its way to a spectacular finish.

SERVE WITH
HERB-CURED FILET OF BEEF WITH HORSERADISH SAUCE

This is an absolutely unique method of pre-cooking beef by coating it with a marinade of lavender and salt and leaving it out in the air to literally "cure." Although it is conceptually hard to leave raw meat out, unrefrigerated, for long hours at a time, the salt is slowly cooking away at the meat, and provides an old-style layer of protection from the elements. It's recommended to use absolutely fresh meat, and as tender as possible. Do not grill or otherwise cook this meat normally, e.g. well done or medium-rare, as the flavors in the herb and salt are so infusive they are only desirable via this process. This stands quite nicely as an entrée, or as a taste treat in a smorgasbord of several other savory delights. As created by chef Robert Grenner, it's daring, it's almost intimidating—but it sure works with this wine! (4 servings)

1 whole beef filet

LAVENDER COATING
2 tablespoons lavender
1 tablespoon salt

HORSERADISH SAUCE
6 oz. freshly grated horseradish
1 tablespoon grainy mustard
$1/4$ teaspoon white pepper
$1 1/2$ Tbl. Worcestershire sauce
$1/3$-$1/2$ cup whole milk

1. Thoroughly pack entire surface of filet of beef with combined lavender-salt mixture. Allow to stand at room temperature for 12-18 hours to cure.
2. Combine horseradish, mustard, pepper, Worcestershire sauce and $1/3$ cup of milk in a blender and purée; if too thick add touches of milk until it reaches a sauce consistency.
3. Lightly coat a sauté pan with non-stick spray, then bring to medium-high heat. Brown the outside of the filet so the coating and the juice of the beef caramelize.
4. Allow to cool.
5. Slice paper thin (a la carpaccio), arrange on a plate.
6. Edge a side of the meat with the sauce, and serve.

THE WINE WITH THIS RECIPE
…finds itself emphatically engaged. The floral characteristics that were latent are brought forward majestically by the lavender, and the pepperishness finds a lasting friend in the horseradish and mustard. The complexity of the wine is gloriously revealed, it's broadened and intensified. The meat is reactive to the flavors in the wine, with absolutely no sense of its being "raw." Aesthetically, even the filet's interior color matches the warm red tone of the wine. These flavors were made to challenge, to coerce, to lure, to be considerable, and they succeed.

1992
ESTATE
BOTTLED

STAG'S LEAP WINE CELLARS

S.L.V.

NAPA VALLEY
CABERNET SAUVIGNON

PRODUCED AND BOTTLED BY
STAG'S LEAP WINE CELLARS, NAPA, CA
ALC. 13.5% BY VOL.
CONTAINS SULFITES

WARREN WINIARSKI

STAG'S LEAP WINE CELLARS CABERNET SAUVIGNON
S.L.V.

...*enjoys a deep, dark, ruby-brick red color, with tons of fruit in the nose, berries, toasted oak, tobacco, voluptuous, classic Cabernet tones. The nose sensations are amplified in the mouth, the balance beautifully secure, as more and more cherry and berry flavors emerge, as the flavors seem to exponentially increase and diversify. Nothing is lost in the finish, as it stamps itself on the surfaces of the mouth to continue its mastery there. An undeniably fantastic, almost flawless wine.*

SERVE WITH

ROAST RACK OF LAMB WITH GRILLED POLENTA,
CABERNET SAUCE AND SEARED VEGETABLES

The good folks at Warren Winiarski's magnificent operation in Napa have provided an entire, three-step meal. As major productions go, this is no slouch, but the end result, when teamed with the elegance of one of the finest wines that Stag's Leap Wine Cellars has to offer, makes the effort well worth it. (4 servings) (Pictured on cover.)

GRILLED POLENTA
3/4 cup polenta
1/4 cup semolina flour
6 cups half-and-half
2 tablespoons vegetable oil
1 tablespoon butter
1 teaspoon white pepper, ground
2 teaspoons salt
1 teaspoon finely chopped sage (optional)
A pinch each of ground cinnamon and ground cloves

RACK OF LAMB
3 pounds lamb rack (12 ribs, ends cleaned for presentation;
    if whole roast to be displayed tie the two ends together
    to form a circle, ribs to the outside—otherwise, just
    slice and serve individual portions)
1/3 cup Pomace olive oil
4 large garlic cloves, chopped
1 tablespoon black pepper, freshly ground
1 1/2 teaspoons rosemary, fresh chopped
1 1/2 teaspoons salt
1 teaspoon thyme, fresh chopped

SAUCE
1 cup red wine (Cabernet Sauvignon)
1 can beef consommé
2 medium shallots, very finely minced
2 tablespoons butter

SEARED VEGETABLES
1 tablespoon peanut oil
1 medium shallot, finely sliced

2 medium zucchinis, halved and sliced on the bias
$1/2$ pound fresh snow peas
12 ripe cherry tomatoes, cut in half
1 teaspoon Balsamic vinegar
$1^1/2$ teaspoons butter
Salt and pepper to taste.

To PREPARE POLENTA
(This should be prepared at least four hours in advance, to allow the cooked polenta time to cool in the refrigerator and set up properly before it is cut and browned.)
1. Bring the half-and-half to a scald. Add the polenta and flour, stirring constantly with a wire whisk. Then, using a wooden spoon, stir the polenta until thick, creamy, and no longer starchy to the taste.
2. Transfer the polenta to a buttered cookie sheet, being careful to spread it to an even thickness of about $3/4$". Place in the refrigerator to cool and set.
3. When set, cut into triangles, then dust each with semolina flour.
4. Heat a skillet over medium-high heat. Add the vegetable oil, then carefully place the polenta in the pan; add the butter and reduce heat to low. When the polenta is a golden brown, flip it over, turn up the heat, and continue the browning on the second side, adding more butter if necessary.

To PREPARE LAMB
1. Preheat oven to 425°F.
2. Mix the olive oil, garlic, and spices by grinding in a molcajete or mortar, then rub the paste over the lamb.
3. Place the lamb in a heavy roasting pan (from which the subsequent sauce will be made), then into the oven. Cook the rack for approximately 25 minutes until the meat reaches an internal temperature of 135°F. Remove the lamb to another tray, cover to keep warm, and allow to rest for 10 minutes while making the sauce.

To PREPARE SAUCE
1. Drain any remaining fat from the roasting pan, then place the pan on the range over high heat.

2. Add the wine, scrape the residue from the pan into the liquid, and boil until reduced by 50%.

3. Add the shallots and cook until almost dry; add the consommé and continue to cook until reduced by 1/3.

4. Turn off the heat, whisk in the butter, adjust the seasoning with salt and pepper, then strain.

TO PREPARE VEGETABLES

1. In a hot skillet or wok, heat peanut oil.

2. Add the shallots and stir briefly; add the zucchini and snow peas, and stir for a minute or two; add the vinegar and tomatoes, and cook for another minute.

3. Reduce heat, add butter; when melted and combined with vegetables, remove from heat, season.

TO SERVE

Slice lamb into serving portions; place lamb on plate, nap with sauce. Serve with the polenta triangles and vegetables.

THE WINE WITH THIS RECIPE

…if possible, becomes even more stunning, bigger, rounder. The alluring tobacco flavor becomes deliciously more prominent, as the thyme and herbs in the sauce helps to elicit the terroir inherent in the wine. A complete composition that gets an A+.

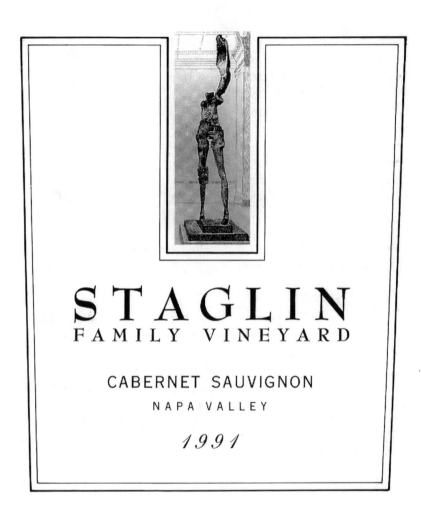

STAGLIN FAMILY VINEYARD CABERNET SAUVIGNON
...is medium-dark and rich in color, with a quality fruit sense in the nose, exhibiting cherry character and soft oak, a pursuasive aroma. The wine goes through a delicious metamorphosis in the glass: immediately full and tannic and inviting, with strong cherry flavor notes early on, it grows and becomes even more engaging as the tobacco appears. An exquisite tasting experience.

SERVE WITH

GRILLED VEAL CHOP WITH GRAINY MUSTARD MARINADE

This is a recipe from the inventive chef Robert Grenner, and takes a delightfully Asian turn to make veal into something even more special. The marinade doubles as a sauce, as you use only a portion of it to influence the veal prior to cooking, with the remainder provided at table to increase the dosage of flavor if desired.

Veal Chops, 1" thick, 1 per person
Marinade:
    1/4 cup grainy mustard
    2 tablespoons lime juice
    1 tablespoon tamari sauce
    1 tablespoon hoisin sauce
    1 tablespoon Worcestershire sauce
    1 tablespoon minced garlic
    1 tablespoon minced ginger
    1/2 teaspoon cayenne pepper

1. Place the chops in a large glass or ceramic dish.
2. Whisk together all the marinade ingredients.
3. Pour enough of the marinade over the meat to cover both sides; reserve the balance.
4. Allow to marinate for 2+ hours at room temperature.
5. Grill the chops on the barbecue until desired doneness. (The meat will cook faster because the marinade will "pre-cook" it a bit).
6. When done, serve; the extra marinade sauce can be served on the side for dipping.

The wine with the recipe
…has its tannins positively boosted, and the fruit almost explodes in the mouth. The completeness of the wine is evident, as the intensity of flavors from the meat and mustard lures more spice and lushness from it. The veal seems to pick up on the changes in the wine as it grows in the glass, matching it stride-for-stride as things develop.

TREFETHEN CABERNET SAUVIGNON

...has a nice, deep dark red color, and reveals wonderful Cabernet aromas—hints of oak, fruit, berry, a slight nod of cigar tobacco. It becomes pleasingly complicated in the mouth, releasing its flavors in a barrage, and in layers. This is a wine of substance, with outstanding tannin structure.

SERVE WITH
GRILLED PORK TENDERLOIN WITH THYME-INFUSED CABERNET SAUCE

The sheer beauty of being able to leave meat on a marinade for an extended period of time, go about your business, and have it so beneficially change its character to match your wine is one of the blessed glories of food; it certainly helps when your wine is as wonderful as Trefethen's. This recipe, obtained via Janet Trefethen, makes good use of their wine and this marinade. Flavors are supposed to talk to each other, and it's clear in this recipe that they speak the same language. (8 servings)

Two pork tenderloins
FOR MARINADE
Whole grain mustard
Salt & Pepper
3 garlic cloves, crushed
6 tablespoons thyme, fresh and chopped (or 3 tablespoons dried)
3 tablespoons good quality Balsamic vinegar
3 tablespoons Cabernet Sauvignon (Trefethen)
FOR SAUCE
1 cup Cabernet Sauvignon (Trefethen)
$1/2$ cup veal or chicken stock
2 tablespoons whole grain mustard
3 tablespoons thyme, fresh and chopped ($1 1/2$ tablespoons dried)

TO PREPARE MARINADE
Make a paste out of the first four ingredients and pat to coat pork tenderloins. Pour liquid over top. Marinate at least 3 hours, or overnight.

TO COOK MEAT
Heat grill or broiler. Grill meat approximately 12 minutes per side to an internal temperature of 135°F. It should be pink when carved. Allow meat to rest a few minutes before serving.

TO MAKE SAUCE
Reduce wine over high heat to $1/2$ volume. Add stock and reduce by one-third. Whisk in mustard. Add thyme just before serving.

THE WINE WITH THIS RECIPE
…becomes a thing of wondrous beauty. As the food and its sauce engage the tannins, the wine turns up its flavors a notch. The sauce plays with the berries, thyme, garlic and Balsamic flavors toy with the tobacco—a thoroughly intriguing association.

DESSERT

Dessert wines are exactly that—usually sweet wines served as a final touch to a fine meal. They come in two basic forms, either a liqueur-like concoction made from a specific sweet-tasting grape variety, such as the Muscat, or as the result of "the noble rot," botrytis cinerea, which occasionally forms on grapes during harvest times after an otherwise unwelcome rain, and which intensifies the sugar content in the grapes but not its acids. The varieties usually used to make such wines are Sauvignon Blanc, Riesling, and Gewürztraminer. Either way, dessert wines tend to be like nectar, thick, rich and wildly flavorful. Not surprisingly, the recipes they are paired with reflect much of these qualities.

HEITZ CELLAR ANGELICA

...is amber-brown in color, and reveals aromas of walnuts, maple syrup and apricots, almost port-like in its presentation. Hints of golden raisins emerge in the mouth, maple syrup, dried fruits, and provides a long, classy finish that clings with its flavors. A gorgeous wine, a cherished experience.

SERVE WITH
TIRAMISU

A traditional Italian dessert, its name literally means "pick-me-up," which is a bright way to regard such a treat. Using a combination of sugared egg yolk and Mascarpone (Italian cream cheese), whipped cream and whipped egg whites, this mixture is tiered with layers of espresso-soaked lady fingers, and capped with decorative pipings of whipped cream, which is finally sprinkled with chocolate shavings. (Milk chocolate? Dark? You decide!) Valentino Restaurant originally provided this version, which we've adapted for general use. With this wonderful wine, made from California's native Mission grapes, it certainly makes for a memorable meal's end. (8 servings)

2+ cups espresso
5 egg yolks
$^1/_8$-$^1/_6$ cup sugar
1 package unflavored gelatin
8 ounces mascarpone (or regular cream cheese)
1 cup heavy cream
4 egg whites
15-20 champagne biscuits (lady fingers)
Chocolate shavings

To prepare ingredients

1. Brew 2 (or more) cups espresso, then when completely cool place in a large flat baking dish for dipping/soaking the biscuits.
2. Mix the egg yolks and sugar well, to ribbon.
3. Blend in the cream cheese bit-by-bit until smooth.
4. Put gelatin in $^1/_8$ cup water (or cold coffee), let sit for a minute, then gently heat until thoroughly dissolved; completely mix into the yolk mixture.
5. Separately beat the whipping cream to a stiff peak—do not over-beat—then divide into two equal parts.
6. Separately beat the egg whites to a stiff peak—again, do not overbeat.
7. Using a scraper, gently fold one part of the the whipped cream into the yolk mix, then follow with the egg whites; be careful not to overmix, so a light wrist is of the utmost.
8. Dip the champagne biscuits into the espresso to soak the outsides, turning them over until a satisfactory brown tinge is obtained overall; because they're spongy, they will be slightly disintegratable, so carefully set them aside on paper towels.

TO ASSEMBLE

1. Place about $1/3$ of the mascarpone mixture in a deep 2-3 quart glass serving bowl.
2. Layer half of the dipped biscuits on top, first encircling and working your way in from the edge until covering it completely.
3. Add another $1/3$ of cream mixture over this layer, then cover again with remainder of soaked biscuits.
4. Top with the last of the cream mixture.
5. Decorate with remaining portion of whipped cream piped through a decorative tip in a pastry bag.
6. Creatively add chocolate shavings to top for color and flavor.
7. Chill at least 2 hours to set; overnight is best.

THE WINE WITH THIS RECIPE

...has its fruit quality heightened immeasurably. The sugar in the dessert eliminates the "alcohol" sense in the wine, as the wine loses its edge and becomes more opulent. A superb dessert wine that is even better with this food.

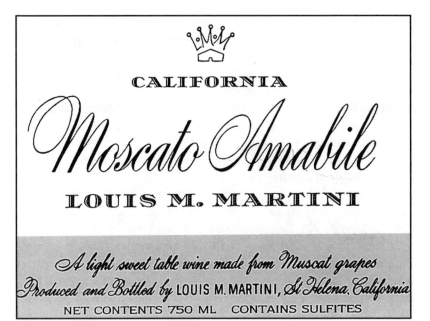

LOUIS M. MARTINI MOSCATO AMABILE

…has a very pale straw color, with a full, bright nose, resplendent with fresh pear and peach aromas, bright and inviting. Not unlike drinking fresh grapes, it also suggests pears, apricots, and peaches. With its frizzante quality, it becomes light and airy while being deeply flavorful, producing a full mouth feel and a finish that avoids being sweet and cloying. This is a completely fresh-tasting wine.

SERVE WITH
AMIABLY SLICED PEARS

The key to this creation of Hendrik Van Leuven's is to have fun differentiating the flavors of the available pear varieties. It is essential to marinate the pears at least 24 hours before serving, as this adds to the beauty and texture of the fruit when served. (If you're really curious, try keeping the pear/marinades separate!) As this wine is frizzante, it's appropriate to serve it in Champagne flutes. (4 servings)

1 each whole pear (D'Anjou, Red Anjou, Bosc, Bartlett), peeled, cored and sliced.
Louis M. Martini Moscato Amabile
Fresh mint leaves

1. Cover the prepared pears with the wine, and let marinate in the refrigerator for 24 hours.
2. To serve, fan out the pear slices in a complete circle, dividing the four varieties into quadrant sections on each serving plate if desired, spoon some of the wine marinade over all, garnish with fresh mint leaves, and accompany with Champagne flutes of the Moscato Amabile.

THE WINE WITH THIS RECIPE

…is a wow! The pear essences in the wine fairly jump out of the glass, with an attractive sweetness that avoids being overly so. A creaminess in the wine emerges, and as the differing pears are sampled they take on a fresh aspect only possible via this method. Not only is this an enticing dessert, it creates fun conversation as the flavors are assessed. A most intriguing meal's end!

Robert Pecota
1994
Moscato d'Andrea
Napa Valley Muscat Blanc

ROBERT PECOTA MOSCATO D'ANDREA

…features a nice, light color. There is a scent of flowers, appropriate to a muscat and true to varietal character. Typically sweet and fruity, there is great balance, a light spiciness, and a slight spryness to its delivery. A supremely enjoyable dessert wine.

SERVE WITH
ZABAGLIONE AND MARINATED FRESH FRUIT

Zabaglione is a simple, rich Italian custard, in this case with Pecota's Moscato replacing the traditional Marsala, which makes for a more light and fruity variation. Kara Pecota Dunn improved this dessert even further by using fresh summer fruit marinated in her father's Moscato. If you love fruit, this one's a winner. (6-8 servings)

1-2 each of any of the following fruits: peaches, pears, apricots, nectarines, pitted or cored, sliced into bite-size segments
1 cup Robert Pecota Moscato d'Andrea
8 egg yolks, lightly whisked
3/4 cup sugar

1. Place prepared fruit in a sealable bag and douse the fruit with 2/3 cup wine; jumble the wine throughout the contents, refrigerate for 12-24 hours.
2. Mix egg yolks, the remaining 1/3 cup wine and sugar together in the top part of a double boiler and cook over rapidly boiling water, whisking constantly until mixture doubles in bulk and thickens.
3. Remove from heat and whisk for another minute.
4. Serve warm or chilled over small bowls of the marinated fruit.

THE WINE WITH THIS RECIPE
...is as if it was prematched on the vine. The tannins in the berries of the dessert gently ease the sweetness from the wine, allowing more intense fruit flavors to emerge. The creaminess of the custard, the grape in the wine, the fresh fruit, all serve each other well. Quite a positive experience!

ACKNOWLEDGMENTS

*S*UCH A COMPLEX project naturally involves a wide range of individuals, without whose help we would not have been able to have gone so far and done so much.

We particularly wish to thank the wineries, restaurants and chefs for their immeasurable contributions.

We also owe a debt of gratitude to Joy Sterling, Greg Friedman, Jim Pollack, Ed Jucksch, Jim Adelman, Harriet Hammond, David and Judy Breitstein, the staff of Duke of Bourbon, Dan and Camila Tosney, Diana Duval, Alicia Paullet, Bill Drewry, Thomas Garcia, Jazmin Garcia, Will Van Leuven, Russell Van Leuven, Chuck and Donna Oken, Jr., Nancy and Bob Klingensmith, Ross Mazzeo, Joe David, and Ray Solley.

APPENDICES

APPENDIX A
VINTAGE INDEX

For the record, this lists the specific vintages of the wines featured in Wine & Dine. This has an extra value in that one might be able to determine how close prior or subsequent vintages maintain consistencies and tendencies as interpreted and presented in the book.

WINERY	YR.	VARIETAL, DESIGNATION
Acacia	1992	Chardonnay, Reserve Carneros
Acacia	1993	Pinot Noir, Reserve Carneros
Au Bon Climat	1993	Pinot Noir, Sanford & Benedict
Au Bon Climat	1993	Chardonnay, Reserve, Sanford & Benedict
Babcock	1991	Sauvignon Blanc, Eleven Oaks Ranch
Babcock	1991	Gewürztraminer
Bonny Doon	1990	Le Cigare Volant
Brander	1993	Sauvignon Blanc, Cuvèe Nicolas
Cakebread Cellars	1991	Chardonnay
Cakebread Cellars	1990	Cabernet Sauvignon
Cakebread Cellars	1992	Sauvignon Blanc
Calera	1991	Pinot Noir, Jensen
Carmenet	1994	Meritage White, Paragon Vineyard
Carmenet	1991	Meritage Red, Moon Mountain
Caymus	1991	Zinfandel
Caymus	1990	Cabernet Sauvignon
Caymus	1989	Cabernet Sauvignon, Special Selection
Chalone	1989	Chardonnay
Chalone	1991	Pinot Blanc
Chateau Montelena	1988	Cabernet Sauvignon
Chateau Montelena	1990	Chardonnay
Diamond Creek	1993	Cabernet Sauvignon, Red Rock Terrace
Domaine Chandon	NV	Brut, Réserve
Domaine Chandon	NV	étoile
Duckhorn	1993	Sauvignon Blanc

Duckhorn	1989	Howell Mountain Red
Duckhorn	1990	Merlot
Edna Valley Vineyard	1991	Chardonnay
Fisher Vineyards	1990	Cabernet Sauvignon, Coach Insignia
Fisher Vineyards	1992	Chardonnay, Coach Insignia
Frog's Leap	1994	Sauvignon Blanc
Girard	1991	Cabernet Sauvignon
Grgich Hills	1988	Cabernet Sauvignon
Grgich Hills	1990	Chardonnay
Grgich Hills	1989	Zinfandel
Grgich Hills	1991	Fumé Blanc
Heitz Cellar	1976	Angelica
Heitz Cellar	1988	Cabernet Sauvignon, Martha's Vineyard
Iron Horse	1991	Brut
Iron Horse	1990	Brut Rosé
Iron Horse	1992	Wedding Cuvée
J (Jordan)	1989	Sparkling Wine
Jordan	1989	Cabernet Sauvignon
Jordan	1990	Chardonnay
Karly	1991	(Notso) Petite Sirah
Kistler	1992	Chardonnay, Dutton Ranch
Long Vineyards	1992	Johannisberg Riesling
Long Vineyards	1994	Sauvignon Blanc
Long Vineyards	1991	Chardonnay
Louis M. Martini	NV	Moscato Amabile
Louis M. Martini	1991	Chardonnay, Reserve
Louis M. Martini	1989	Cabernet Sauvignon, Reserve
Louis M. Martini	1993	Gewürztraminer
Martin Bros.	1991	Cabernet Etrusco
Mayacamas	1987	Cabernet Sauvignon
Nalle	1993	Zinfandel
Ojai Vineyard	1993	Syrah
Opus One	1989	Meritage Red
Qupé	1993	Syrah, Bien Nacido Reserve
Ridge	1990	Cabernet Sauvignon, Monte Bello
Ridge	1991	Zinfandel, Lytton Springs
Robert Mondavi Winery	1991	Fumé Blanc, Reserve
Robert Mondavi Winery	1991	Pinot Noir, Reserve
Robert Mondavi Winery	1991	Chardonnay, Reserve
Robert Mondavi Winery	1990	Cabernet Sauvignon, Reserve

Robert Pecota	1992	Moscato d'Andrea
Robert Pecota	1991	Merlot, Steven Andre Vineyard
Robert Pecota	1990	Cabernet Sauvignon, Kara's Vineyard
Robert Pecota	1992	Sauvignon Blanc
S. Anderson	1990	Brut
Sanford	1991	Chardonnay, Barrel Select
Sanford	1992	Pinot Noir
Schramsberg	1988	Crémant
Schramsberg	1989	Brut Rosé
Schramsberg	1987	Blanc de Noirs
Simi	1989	Cabernet Sauvignon
Simi	1991	Chardonnay
Spottswoode	1990	Cabernet Sauvignon
Spottswoode	1992	Sauvignon Blanc
Stag's Leap Wine Cellars	1990	Cabernet Sauvignon, FAY
Stag's Leap Wine Cellars	1990	Cabernet Sauvignon, SLV
Stag's Leap Wine Cellars	1990	Petite Sirah
Staglin Family Vineyard	1988	Cabernet Sauvignon
Stonestreet	1992	Pinot Noir
Storybook Mountain	1992	Zinfandel
Talley	1993	Pinot Noir
Trefethen	1994	White Riesling
Trefethen	1992	Cabernet Sauvignon
Wild Horse	1992	Chardonnay
Wild Horse	1991	Pinot Noir

APPENDIX B
SAUCE BASES

STOCK

Although there are countless stock recipes, Michael's Restaurant provided one that we think is a remarkable and appropriate inclusion. Do not underestimate the value of stock.

MICHAEL'S STOCK
5 pounds chicken, squab, duck, rabbit, veal, or lamb bones
1 tablespoon unsalted butter
1 large yellow onion, peeled and cut in half
1 cup dry red wine (non-chicken only)

2 gloves garlic, unpeeled
1 tablespoon whole white peppercorns
2 bay leaves
2 carrots, coarsely chopped
1/2 stalk celery, including leaves, coarsely chopped
2 sprigs fresh thyme
1/2 bunch fresh tarragon
1/2 bunch fresh basil

Bone preparation:
For chicken stock, leave the chicken bones unroasted; for all others, place the bones in a roasting pan and roast the bones in a 325°F oven until deep golden brown, 1 1/2 - 2 hours.

To make stock:
1. Melt the butter in a heavy skillet over medium-to-low heat and sauté the onion halves until caramel-brown all over, 15-20 minutes per side.
2. If chicken is used, place the bones and onion in a large stockpot and go to Step 3. For all others, place the roasted bones in a large stockpot with the onion; deglaze the roasting pan with the wine over low heat, scraping the elements loose, then add this wine to the stockpot.
3. Put all the remaining ingredients in the stockpot and add enough water to cover. Bring the water to a boil over medium heat, skimming the surface as necessary, then reduce the heat and simmer, skimming often, for about 5 hours. (Walk away, do other things, run errands, whatever, come back, check in, skim, don't let it evaporate too much, enjoy the smell as it permeates the house, and be assured you're doing a good thing.)
4. When done, let cool.
5. Remove and discard the major heavyweights. Pour the stock through a double thickness of cheesecloth to remove solids.
6. Let the stock cool to room temperature, then refrigerate until cold.
7. Lift or spoon off any fat that has risen and congealed on top before using.

Storage:
Use freezer bags marked with what kind of stock and how many cups for easy reference. Ice cubes of stock are also handy for quick, incidental use, which can be stored in a large freezer bag as well.

BROWN SAUCE

To a certain extent, brown sauce is doubly concentrated beef stock, with some added influences to create a luxurious base. Canned condensed versions are readily available. Any recipe calling for brown sauce throughout this book employed the version cited in the venerable kitchen standard *Joy of Cooking* by Rombauer and Becker, and which takes about 2-2½ hours to prepare.

½ cup beef or veal drippings
1 cup mirepoix (diced carrots, onion, celery heart ribs, ½ crushed bay leaf, sprig of thyme, simmered in 1 tablespoon butter, then deglazed with Madeira)
½ cup flour
10 black peppercorns
2 cups drained, peeled tomatoes or 2 cups tomato purée
½ cup coarsely chopped parsley
8 cups rich beef stock

Melt the drippings in a heavy saucepan, then add the mirepoix. When it begins to color, add the flour and stir until it is thoroughly browned. Add the peppercorns, tomatoes and parsley, mix well, then add the stock. Simmer until reduced by half, stir occasionally and skim off the fat as it rises. As it cools, strain and stir occasionally to prevent skin from forming; the sauce should be the consistency of whipping cream, no thicker.

DEMI-GLAZE SAUCE

This takes the above-mentioned brown sauce and intensifies it even more through further reduction. Again, *Joy of Cooking* provided the procedure which was followed in the creation of any recipes calling for this rich sauce.

4 cups Brown Sauce
4 cups rich beef stock, flavored with mushroom trimmings
½ cup dry sherry

Combine the sauce and stock in a heavy saucepan, simmer slowly until reduced by half. Strain into a double boiler and keep warm over hot water while adding the sherry.

APPENDIX C
CHILI POWDER

It's actually quite easy to make fresh powder from any dried chiles, and with the wide range now available there's much experimentation possible. However, be careful to thoroughly wash your hands whenever you touch the chiles—it's amazing how casually one can rub an eye without thinking, and the pain that the slightest touch of chile residue can cause is *excrutiating*.

1 ounce dried chiles (Negro for Ridge Zinfandel, California for Ojai Syrah)

1. Break the pods open, remove the seeds and the veins.
2. Bake in the oven at 450°F until crisp, or microwave on high for 20-30 seconds. Be aware that the fumes this creates can be very potent, so place the plate of just-baked pods under a vent until they subside.
3. Place the crisp pod pieces in a spice grinder, and grind until a fine powder is created.

INDEX